"Poul Rohleder has gifted the mental health profession with a superb volume, exploring the much-overlooked and often misunderstood concept of the Oedipus complex. Written with much clarity and concision and with tremendous historical accuracy, the author has investigated numerous psychoanalytical perspectives and, also, has explored the impact of contemporary views regarding gender and sexual orientation. I recommend this book warmly to every single psychological worker."

Professor Brett Kahr, *Senior Fellow, Tavistock Institute of Medical Psychology, London; Visiting Professor of Psychoanalysis and Mental Health, Regent's University London; and Honorary Director of Research, Freud Museum London*

The Oedipus Complex

In this book, Poul Rohleder presents a comprehensive and accessible introduction to the theory of the Oedipus complex and its standing in contemporary psychoanalysis.

The Oedipus Complex: A Contemporary Introduction charts the developments of the theory, exploring Freud's original work on the subject before moving on to later developments by Klein and the Independents in the UK. Rohleder interweaves perspectives from French psychoanalysis and contemporary relational thought, and explores the various critiques of the theory, including feminist, queer, and cross-cultural perspectives. Through this holistic and contemporary exploration, Rohleder offers the contemporary practitioner a broad and nuanced consideration of how Oedipal dynamics can play a vital role in their work with patients.

This book will be of interest to psychoanalysts and psychotherapists in practice and training who have an interest in expanding their understanding of the Oedipus complex and its relevance to a contemporary way of working.

Poul Rohleder is a Clinical Psychologist and Psychoanalytic Psychotherapist in private practice in central London, UK. He is a Senior Member of the British Psychotherapy Foundation and an Honorary Senior Lecturer at the Department of Psychosocial and Psychoanalytic Studies, University of Essex, UK.

Routledge Introductions to Contemporary Psychoanalysis

Series Editor: Aner Govrin
Executive Editor: Yael Peri Herzovich

Erotic Transferences: A Contemporary Introduction
Andrea Celenza

Otto Kernberg: A Contemporary Introduction
Frank Yeomans, Diana Diamond, Eve Caligor

Erich Fromm: A Contemporary Introduction
Sandra Buechler

Narcissism: A Contemporary Introduction
Richard Wood

The Death Drive: A Contemporary Introduction
Rossella Valdrè

Depression: A Contemporary Introduction
Marianne Leuzinger-Bohleber

Ronald Fairbairn: A Contemporary Introduction
David P. Celani

Depression: A Contemporary Introduction
Marianne Leuzinger-Bohleber

Ronald Fairbairn: A Contemporary Introduction
David P. Celani

The Evidence for Psychodynamic Psychotherapy: A Contemporary Introduction
Kevin McCarthy, Carla Capone and Liat Leibovich

Psychoanalytic Group Psychotherapy: A Contemporary Introduction
Richard M. Billow

Existential Psychoanalysis: A Contemporary Introduction
M. Guy Thompson

Dreams and Dream Interpretation: A Contemporary Introduction
Christian Roesler

Interpersonal Psychoanalysis: A Contemporary Introduction
Anna Maria Loiacono

Psychodynamic and Psychoanalytic Supervision: A Contemporary Introduction
Christine Driver

Couple Relations: A Contemporary Introduction
Mary Morgan

The Oedipus Complex: A Contemporary Introduction
Poul Rohleder

Psychoanalytic Film Theory: A Contemporary Introduction
Ben Tyrer

Thomas Ogden: A Contemporary Introduction
Ofrit Shapira-Berman

For more information about this series, please visit: www.routledge.com/Routledge-Introductions-to-Contemporary-Psychoanalysis/book-series/ICP

The Oedipus Complex

A Contemporary Introduction

Poul Rohleder

Routledge
Taylor & Francis Group

LONDON AND NEW YORK

Designed cover image: © Michal Heiman, Asylum 1855–2020,
The Sleeper (video, psychoanalytic sofa and Plate 34), exhibition
view, Herzliya Museum of Contemporary Art, 2017

First published 2026
by Routledge
4 Park Square, Milton Park, Abingdon, Oxon OX14 4RN

and by Routledge
605 Third Avenue, New York, NY 10158

*Routledge is an imprint of the Taylor & Francis Group, an informa
business*

British Library Cataloguing-in-Publication Data
A catalogue record for this book is available from the British
Library

ISBN: 978-1-032-49572-9 (hbk)
ISBN: 978-1-032-49565-1 (pbk)
ISBN: 978-1-003-39447-1 (ebk)

DOI: 10.4324/9781003394471

Typeset in Times New Roman
by Taylor & Francis Books

Contents

Series Editor's Preface   x
ANER GOVRIN

1   Introduction   1

2   Freud's Theory of the Oedipus Complex   7

3   Klein and the Oedipal Situation   20

4   Feminist Critiques of the Oedipus Complex   34

5   Perspectives from French Psychoanalysis   51

6   Relational Perspectives on the Oedipus Complex   65

7   Challenging Heteronormativity   86

8   Culture and the Oedipus Complex   101

9   Oedipus Now   113

References   118
Index   125

Series Editor's Preface

Routledge Introductions to Contemporary Psychoanalysis is one of the most prominent psychoanalytic publishing ventures of our day. The series' aim is to become an encyclopedia of psychoanalysis, with each entry given its own book.

This comprehensive series illuminates the intricate landscape of psychoanalytic theory and practice. In this collection of concise yet illuminating volumes, we delve into the influential figures, groundbreaking concepts, and transformative theories that shape the contemporary psychoanalytic landscape.

At the heart of each volume lies a commitment to clarity, accessibility, and depth. Our expert authors, renowned scholars and practitioners in their respective fields, guide readers through the complexities of psychoanalytic thought with precision and enthusiasm. Whether you are a seasoned psychoanalyst, a student eager to explore the field, or a curious reader seeking insight into the human psyche, our series offers a wealth of knowledge and insight.

Each volume serves as a gateway into a specific aspect of psychoanalytic theory and practice. From the pioneering works of Sigmund Freud to the innovative contributions of modern theorists such as Antonino Ferro and Michal Eigen, our series covers a diverse range of topics, including seminal figures, key concepts, and emerging trends. Whether you are interested in classical psychoanalysis, object relations theory, or the intersection of neuroscience and psychoanalysis, you will find a wealth of resources within our collection.

One of the hallmarks of our series is its interdisciplinary approach. While rooted in psychoanalytic theory, our volumes draw upon insights from psychology, philosophy, sociology, and other disciplines to offer a holistic understanding of the human mind and its complexities.

Each volume in the series is crafted with the reader in mind, balancing scholarly rigor with engaging prose. Whether you are embarking on your journey into psychoanalysis or seeking to deepen your understanding of specific topics, our series provides a clear and comprehensive roadmap.

Moreover, our series is committed to fostering dialogue and debate within the psychoanalytic community. Each volume invites readers to critically engage with the material, encouraging reflection, discussion, and further exploration.

We invite you to join us on this journey of discovery as we explore the ever-evolving landscape of psychoanalysis.

Aner Govrin

Chapter 1

Introduction

A girl, aged 4 or 5, is lying in her father's arms, cuddled up against his chest, crying. She is telling her mother (who is filming her), that she's upset because she "can't marry anybody". "Why? What happened?", we hear her mother ask. Because "YOU married him! So now I can't marry him" she says in sobs of tears, referring to her mother having married her father. The girl is devastated. Turning to her father, she says "and YOU married mom". "Why?!" she asks, upset and angry at this injustice. "I can't believe you married MY dad!", she cries.

This humorous YouTube video (@carrfamily6645; November 1, 2021), touchingly depicts the girl's feelings of exclusion and betrayal related to what we might call her Oedipus complex – the desire for one parent and rivalry towards the other. Sigmund Freud's theory of the Oedipus complex is one of the most important theoretical concepts in psychoanalysis, and one of the most contested. Its relevance keeps on being questioned, mostly outside the profession of psychoanalysis, but also within. Yet, parents can make anecdotal reports of comments made by children like those shown in this YouTube video, that demonstrate how common these sorts of fantasies and feelings are. At the time of writing this book, two separate theatre productions of *Oedipus* were showing on London's West End. The emotional and relational themes of the story of Oedipus resonate widely.

Freud's first recorded thoughts about the Oedipus complex were written in a letter to his friend, Wilhem Fliess, dated October 15, 1897. In this letter he reflects on his own self-analysis (which later

DOI: 10.4324/9781003394471-1

informed his great work, *The Interpretation of Dreams*) and he states: "A single idea of general value dawned on me. I have found, in my own case too, being in love with my mother and jealous of my father, and I now consider it a universal event in early childhood" (Masson, 1985, p. 272).

Freud went on to regard the Oedipus complex, characterised by the child's conflicts between their desire for the opposite-sex parent, the taboo against incest and fear of castration, as universal and as central to understanding human psychological development. He took the Greek myth of Oedipus, as depicted in three plays written by Sophocles, as providing a template for the Oedipus complex.

Oedipus was the son of King Laius and Queen Jocasta, rulers of Thebes. Laius had had desires for and was accused of having raped Chrysippus, the son of Pelops, the King of Pisa. Because of this alleged crime, Pelops laid a curse on Laius (unbeknownst to him) that if he were to have children, he would be killed by his own son. Laius later became King of Thebes and married Jocasta. Thebes was experiencing a devastating plague, and Laius and Jocasta consulted the Oracle of Apollo at Delphi, who told Laius that the plague was due to their family being cursed, and that he will be murdered by his son, who will later marry Jocasta. Jocasta later gives birth to a baby boy, and in a desperate attempt to thwart the prophecy, Laius commands that the infant be killed. He disables the baby, by piercing his ankles, and orders a shepherd to take him and leave him out on a mountainside to die. However, the shepherd takes pity on the baby, and gives him to another shepherd, who takes the baby boy to the city of Corinth, where he is adopted by King Polybus and Queen Merope. They name the boy Oedipus, which means 'swollen foot', because of the injuries inflicted on his ankles.

Oedipus had a happy childhood in Corinth, unaware of his origins, until one day a man questioned his paternity, and he received evasive answers from Polybus and Merope. Puzzled by this, Oedipus consults the Oracle, who informs him of the curse that he is fated to kill his father and marry his mother. Horrified by what he is told, and still believing Polybus and Merope to be his parents, he flees Corinth and travels towards Thebes. On his way, he encounters an old man travelling with an entourage, who runs Oedipus off the road. An argument ensues, and in anger, Oedipus kills the man and his entourage. After a long journey, Oedipus finally arrives at Thebes, which is once again gripped by a devastating plague, inflicted by the Sphinx, a monster with the body of a lion, head of a woman and wings of an eagle. The Sphinx states that it will save the city of the plague if someone can answer a riddle. The king of Thebes, Laius, has been killed, and his brother, Creon, promises the throne and the hand of Queen Jocasta to whoever can solve the riddle of the Sphinx. Oedipus manages to solve it, and the city is saved. As promised to him, Oedipus becomes King and marries Jocasta.

Some years later, the city of Thebes is in the grips of a plague once again. King Oedipus, determined to save his city from the destructive plague, sends Creon to consult with the Oracle. Creon returns informing Oedipus of the Oracle's message: the plague will only be lifted and the city saved if the murder of King Laius, who was mysteriously killed on the road, is solved and the murderer punished. Eager to uncover the truth of Laius' murder, Oedipus orders an investigation, and summons the seer Tiresias, who possesses the gift of prophecy. Tiresias is at first reluctant to tell Oedipus the truth but eventually suggests that Oedipus himself is the killer being sought. Oedipus at first dismisses this revelation as part of a plot against him orchestrated by Creon and Tiresias. Jocasta meanwhile starts to remember the old prophecy told to her and Laius: that their son will kill his father and marry his mother. She believes this prophecy was thwarted because they had left their son to die. Jocasta lets Oedipus know about this, in an effort to persuade him as to the falsehood of Tiresias claims. Eventually, the pieces are put together and Oedipus and Jocasta learn the truth: that Oedipus killed his father and married his mother. The old prophecy had indeed been fulfilled. Jocasta, devastated by the truth, hangs herself in shame and grief. Oedipus, overwhelmed with guilt and despair, gouges his eyes out, blinding himself.

The myth of Oedipus is a rich, detailed story. Freud was interested primarily in one aspect, that Oedipus killed his father and married his mother, regarding it as a template for a universal truth about sexuality and the taboo against incest. Other aspects of the story have also been taken note of, such as the 'crimes' committed by Laius and Jocasta, rendering Oedipus a victim of these crimes, rather than a perpetrator, as well as the attempts by Oedipus and Jocasta herself to dismiss the truth as it began to be revealed.

The validity and the centrality of Freud's theory of the Oedipus complex has been questioned and challenged numerous times. Furthermore, what is referred to as the 'Oedipus complex', most typically a reference to the boy's incestuous wish towards his mother and parricidal wishes towards his father, is made even more complex by different attempts to formulate variations that include accounts of female sexuality, and of same-sex desire. Within the developmental history of psychoanalytic theory, Freud's Oedipus complex has been challenged, supported, revised, and revisited many times over. Yet, it endures.

This book attempts to provide an introduction to the Oedipus complex and some of the major developments and revisions on Freud's original theories, as well as some key critiques made. It is beyond the scope of an introductory book to cover all that has been written. Out of necessity, I have had to be selective, and I have chosen to mostly stick to psychoanalytic writers. I have structured the book into seven chapters that introduce some of the important theoretical developments and revisions on Freud's initial theory of the Oedipus complex. Chapter 2 outlines Freud's theories of the male and the female Oedipus complex, and his concepts of innate bisexuality and the 'complete' Oedipus complex, with some introduction to key points of critique. Chapter 3 introduces the important revisions made by Melanie Klein that focused on early dynamics of the Oedipus complex in the first year of life, and contributions from contemporary Kleinian psychoanalysts that highlight the triangular situation between child and parents. In Chapter 4 some key revisions made from feminist perspectives are discussed, particularly critiques of the phallic-centric formulation of Freud, and suggestions of alternative Oedipal theories that capture the unique aspects of female sexuality. Chapter 5 introduces some important perspectives from French psychoanalysis, in particular the work of Lacan and Laplanche, that considers the importance of unconscious communication from the adult for the developing sexuality of the child. In Chapter 6 the work of different psychoanalysts that offers more relational perspectives on the parent–child relationship and the

Oedipus complex is discussed. Theoretical contributions that challenge the heteronormative formulations of the Oedipus complex are discussed in Chapter 7, offering a more 'positive' account of same-sex desire and homosexuality. Freud's ideas about innate bisexuality are revisited here. Chapter 8 explores some cross-cultural investigations of the Oedipus complex, and challenges to Freud's suggestion that castration anxiety and the taboo against incest are universal and biologically innate. In a final chapter (Chapter 9) I offer some thoughts to bring some key ideas together and discuss recent contributions from neuroscience that might offer a useful contemporary biological account of the Oedipus complex. I have used this structure simply as a way to organise the material, and it is not intended to depict clearly defined distinctions, nor a chronological order.

Many different terms are used to describe the cluster of conflicts that Freud described as the Oedipus complex, such as 'Oedipus situation', or 'Oedipal phase' or period, or reference to 'triadic' or 'triangular' relationships, situations, or dynamics. I will use the terms used by specific theorists and will use some of these interchangeably. I approach thinking about the 'Oedipus complex' as broadly describing the cluster of conflicting feelings of love and hate that a child experiences in relation to his or her parents, and the triangular relationships involved that a child must navigate their way through and find their place in the family and in the social world. I have used the terms used in the psychoanalytic literature I am drawing on, and at times such language denotes pathologising or problematic views that may not reflect a contemporary approach. I refer to 'homosexuality' and 'homosexual' when referring to same-sex desire as these are the terms most used, mindful though that many regard these terms as the language of diagnosis. The book includes some clinical material in Chapters 4 and 7. These are concisely written and are intended to illustrate some of the Oedipal dynamics discussed in the chapter, rather than to provide a detailed account of a way of working. These are composite case studies built on different experiences and themes from my clinical work over the past two decades, and work heard in supervision.

Note that in this book I draw on *The Standard Edition of the Complete Psychological Works of Sigmund Freud* translated and edited by James Strachey. However, there is now the *Revised Standard Edition*, translated and edited by Mark Solms.

Chapter 2

Freud's Theory of the Oedipus Complex

Freud developed a *psychosexual* theory of human development and considered the Oedipus complex as fundamental to understanding the development of sexual and gender identity and personality. In this chapter I provide an outline of Freud's theory of the Oedipus complex as it pertains to males and to females, and his accounts of both male and female heterosexuality and homosexuality. I will then discuss his ideas about innate bisexuality and the 'complete' Oedipus complex, which are concepts also taken up in later chapters. Finally, I will point out some key points of critique that are explored in more detail in other chapters. It will be helpful to first briefly situate the Oedipus complex within his broader theory of infantile sexuality and psychosexual development.

Infantile Sexuality and Psychosexual Development

Freud (1905) regarded sexuality as something instinctual that develops from within the individual, observing the existence of infantile sexuality and its development into adult sexuality. By 'infantile sexuality', he referred to the experience of pleasure and bodily excitation in various regions of the body. With the onset of puberty, infantile sexuality develops into genital sexuality and later into adult sexual behaviour.

Freud's theory of sexuality was first laid out in his *Three Essays on Sexuality* (1905), where he described the sexual instinct, and infantile sexuality, as initially "polymorphously perverse" (p. 191), in that pleasure (as derived from the sexual instinct) can be

DOI: 10.4324/9781003394471-2

experienced in many areas of the body and in relation to various objects. He observed the sexual instinct as expressed in the sensation of pleasure and gratification concentrated in the various erotogenic zones of the body: the skin, the mucous membranes of the mouth and the anus, and, with the onset of puberty, the genitals. In revisions he made to the *Three Essays* in 1915, Freud added a description of three key phases of psychosexual development, the oral, anal, and genital phases, and a fourth stage of latency between infancy and puberty, where the sexual instinct is largely supressed. In a footnote added in 1924, Freud included reference to the phallic stage of development (p. 199). Thus, Freud understood psychosexual development as passing through five sequential stages, covering the ages from birth through childhood, puberty, and adolescence and into adulthood: The oral stage, the anal stage, the phallic stage, the latency stage, and the genital stage. These stages are named as such with reference to erotogenic zones of the body where the sexual instinct and the resulting experience of pleasure is most concentrated as the child develops.

According to Freud, the oral stage of psychosexual development occurs during the first year of life. In this stage, the sexual instinct is focused on the mouth, where pleasure is derived primarily through the activity of sucking – sucking the mother's breast or a teat of a baby-bottle, the baby sucking their thumb or hand or other objects. The anal stage occurs during the second and third years of life, where the sexual instinct is more concentrated on the anal zone. The young toddler experiences pleasure through the sensations of their bowel movements, through the retention or passing of their stools. This is usually the period of toilet training, which also constitutes a process where the child must begin to renounce some of his or her instinctual pleasures, as the primary caregivers place limits on the child's uninhibited behaviours. During the phallic stage of psychosexual development (occurring during years 3 to 6), the young child discovers their genitals and the experience of infantile masturbatory pleasure, as well as becoming aware of the anatomical differences between the sexes. It is during this period that the child experiences the Oedipus complex in relation to their parents, and experiences castration anxiety and a taboo of incest (more about this below). After the drama of the phallic stage and the Oedipus complex, the latency stage (between the ages of 6 and 11) represents a period of relative quiet in terms of sexuality. The child, having a more developed superego, has a greater capacity to control and supress his or her sexual instinct, and it becomes sublimated onto other activities, typically the formation of friendships, playing games and sport, and learning activities. Freud, writing at the very start of the twentieth century, might have formulated the latency stage as a period of sexual 'quiet', observing the mannered behaviours of children at the time. In modern times, contemporary psychotherapists and psycho-analysts have recognised the greater sexual "blatancy" (Lemma, 2017, p. 44) of childhood, with the sexualisation of clothing, media, and culture. The final stage of psychosexual development is the genital stage, which begins at puberty. This is a period of great emotional drama, as the sexual instinct re-emerges in full force and the conflicts of the Oedipal stage are revived as the child develops and experiences desire towards an object among their peer group, and feelings of hostility towards competing rivals. In this final stage, the 'polymorphously perverse' sexuality of infancy has now developed into a more orientated adult genital sexuality.

The Oedipus Complex

Freud developed his theory of the Oedipus complex in later publications and presented it in some depth in *The Ego and the Id* (1923). His theory of the Oedipus complex provided more of an organising framework for sexuality than was first articulated in his first edition of the *Three Essays*, which made no mention of the Oedipus complex, and only included some minor content in his third revision (Van Haute & Westerink, 2020).

In *Totem and Taboo*, Freud (1913) also suggested that the Oedipus complex, particularly the experience of castration anxiety and the taboo against incest, is phylogenetically inherited. That is, they are innate evolutionary-biological dispositions that conflict with the child's desire towards his primary object (the male child's incestuous desire towards his mother). In *Totem and Taboo*, he described the murder of the primal father by the primal horde, and the establishment of the incest taboo as a universal law. He regarded this as the basis for the establishment of civilisation, society, and culture. I will discuss this in more detail in Chapter 8 rather than here, as it also pertains to ideas about culture.

Freud (1923, 1924, 1925) wrote with much more detail about the Oedipus complex for the male child, rather than the female child, and with more emphasis on heterosexual orientation, rather than homosexual or bisexual orientation. He referred to the heterosexual formulation as the 'positive' Oedipus complex, and the homosexual formulation as the 'negative' Oedipus complex, reflecting the naming of homosexuality as 'inversion' at that time.

The Boy's Oedipus Complex

Due to the intimacy of breastfeeding and its pleasures for the infant, the mother is the first object of desire for both the boy and the girl. During the phallic stage of psychosexual development, the child observes that there are anatomical differences between the sexes. Freud regarded the penis as central to the child's understanding of 'masculine' and 'feminine' – males possess a penis, and females seem to lack one. At first Freud suggested that the male child assumes that everyone has a penis, and thus that the mother too possesses a penis. The sight of the absence of a penis in girls and women is experienced as a kind of trauma for the boy, who interprets this absence as being the result of castration. I recall a friend of mine telling a group of us how her young son asked her, with some concern, why his baby sister did not have a 'willy', asking her why 'God' had not given her one; was it because he was angry? According to Freud, the boy comes to fear the loss of his own penis through similar castration. The boy sees the father as a rival for his mother's affection, and fears retaliation by the bigger, more powerful father. Thus, castration anxiety is not simply due to the observation of the anatomical differences between the sexes but is linked to the fantasy of punishment for incestuous desire.

A wonderfully amusing example of the typical Oedipal desires and rivalries of a young boy comes from the writer Frank O'Connor. In his short story, *My Oedipus Complex* (1933/2005), he describes a 5-year-old boy's jealousy and feelings of exclusion when 'Daddy' returns from fighting in World War I, and his mother starts telling him not to interrupt them when she is busy talking to 'Daddy'. Larry, the young boy, observes how this seems to happen much too often for his liking:

> At tea-time, 'talking to Daddy' began again, complicated this time by the fact that he had an evening paper, and every few minutes he put it down and told Mother something new out of it. I felt this was foul play. Man for man, I was prepared to compete with him any time for Mother's attention, but when he had it all made up for him by other people it left me no chance. Several times I tried to change the subject without success.

> 'You must be quiet while Daddy is reading, Larry', Mother said impatiently.

> It was clear that she either genuinely liked talking to Father better than talking to me, or else that he had some terrible hold on her which made her afraid to admit the truth.
>   'Mummy', I said that night when she was tucking me up, 'do you think if I prayed hard God would send Daddy back to the war?'

> (pp. 14–15)

The short story humorously describes Larry's anger at, and rivalry with, his father, whose return home from the war disturbs the "most peaceful period" (p. 12) of his life when it was just him and his mother. Things become even more challenging for Larry when a new baby arrives and takes away even more of his mother's attention and affection!

As a result of castration anxiety, the male child must renounce his desire for his mother, accept that he is a child and not an adult, and identify with his father, becoming like him in order to one day attract a female partner of his own. This resolution of the Oedipus complex establishes the taboo against incest, which Freud at first regarded as a "cultural demand" (1905, p. 225) placed on the child. The superego develops out of the resolution of the Oedipus complex, as the child internalises their parents' rules and, through them, society's moral laws about sexuality, sex roles, and intergenerational differences (Freud, 1925). What starts in the phallic stage, re-emerges during puberty, where the adolescent experiences sexual desire and seeks out intimate, romantic relationships with a partner their own age (rather than their parent), and develops a stronger sense of sexual identity and orientation, which matures in adulthood. The infantile libidinal Oedipal conflicts in relation to the parents are repressed, and destroyed (Freud, 1924), in favour of the internalisation of parental authority.

Male Homosexuality

Freud regarded homosexuality as a possible outcome of the Oedipus complex but seemed to have some difficulty in theorising male homosexuality definitively. Lewes (1988) outlines different etiological theories formulated by Freud in his various writings, which at times relate and at other times contradict with each other. One theory, described in his *Three Essays* (Freud, 1905) as well as in his case study on Leonardo da Vinci (Freud, 1910), suggests that the development of the boy who later becomes homosexual is a result of a very close libidinal bond with his mother, with a more distant father. Rather than relinquish this libidinal tie to the mother, he identifies with her and seeks a partner who is like him (i.e. a male partner). He describes this as a narcissistic object choice, as Leonardo's sexual object is (indirectly) himself. Although the libidinal tie to the mother is relinquished in reality, it is preserved at an unconscious level.

In a second theory, described in his case study of Little Hans, Freud (1909) suggests that homosexuality develops as a result of the male child withdrawing his incestuous desire from his mother, whom he viewed with horror and disgust as a castrated figure. Fearing castration, he turns his desire instead to a compromise figure, an effeminate male partner; "a 'woman with a penis'" (Lewes, 1988, p. 36), thus ensuring that the phallic is maintained.

The theory that Freud regarded as outlining the most common explanation for homosexuality is what is known as the 'negative' Oedipus complex. This theory was examined in Freud's analysis of the childhood neurosis of the 'Wolf Man' (1918). Freud understood that the Wolf Man's heterosexual identification with his father was undone following a seduction of sexual play by his older sister. The boy turned away from his sister towards his governess, who one day threatened him with castration when he had showed her his penis. This castration anxiety led to the development of a passive "feminine attitude" (p. 64), at first with his sister and governess, and then with his father. This coincided with a dream that referred to an earlier witnessing of the 'primal scene' (Freud suspected that the boy had seen his parents having sex), and the boy's wish to be penetrated by his father. Fearing castration for this sexual wish, the boy represses his sexual desire for his father, recovers his masculine identification with him, and makes a heterosexual object choice. In this formulation, Freud observed the possibility of shifting masculine/active and feminine/passive libidinal positions and a psychic bisexuality, and a co-occurring positive and negative Oedipal conflict in an individual. This is discussed further below.

It is important to note that while some of Freud's writing on homosexuality, and the terminology he used, may be read as problematic, and formulated in heteronormative terms, Freud did not regard homosexuality as a perversion or a psychopathology. He understood a homosexual object choice as just as valid an outcome of the Oedipus complex. In a footnote in the *Three Essays*, he suggests that "all human beings are capable of making a homosexual object-choice and have in fact made one in their unconscious" (1905, p. 144). Despite Freud's clarity about this, later psychoanalysts took up a more pathologising view of homosexuality as involving a failure of a 'healthy' resolution of the Oedipus complex.

The Girl's Oedipus Complex

Freud (1926) regarded female sexuality as something of a "dark continent" (p. 212), and his theory of female sexuality was less developed than his theory of male sexuality. As noted above, Freud regarded the phallus as central to the development of male and female sexuality, viewing the development of female sexuality as revolving around her perceived 'lack' of a penis. As with the male child, the female child's sexual instinct is more strongly directed towards the mother, but her libidinal attachment to her mother is of longer duration than that of the boy's (Freud, 1931).

Freud (1931) suggested that the little girl starts off as being like a boy, equating her clitoris as a rudimentary penis, and adopting a masculine position in relation to her desires for the mother. According to Freud (1926, 1931) the girl has no awareness of her vagina at this stage, only discovering it in puberty. During the phallic stage of development, the girl observes the anatomical differences between the sexes, and that she does not have a penis, at least not one as large as the boy's. Freud states:

> The little girl's clitoris behaves just like a penis to begin with; but, when she makes a comparison with a playfellow of the other sex, she perceives that she has 'come off badly' and she feels this as a wrong done to her and as a ground for inferiority.

> (1924, p. 178)

Thus, the little girl sees herself as already castrated. She also learns that her mother lacks a penis and feels disappointed in her as a castrated woman who is unable to help her get a penis. The girl develops 'penis envy', and renounces her affection for her mother, and turns her desire to her father, who is the possessor of the penis, wishing to have a baby with him. The baby becomes a symbol for a penis which she can now possess, which Freud referred to as an "equation 'penis-child'" (1925, p. 256). However, because of the incest taboo, she realises the impossibility of this, and renounces her desire for her father, returning her affections back to the mother but by identifying with her (the object of father's affection) and seeking an opposite-sex partner, like her father, with whom she can one day have a baby.

According to Freud, the Oedipus complex is resolved differently for males and for females. For males it is via castration anxiety, and for females it is via penis envy. The difference being that for boys, castration is threatened, whereas for the girl, castration has already happened, and it is castration anxiety that propels the Oedipus complex for the girl (Freud, 1925). For this reason, he suggested that the Oedipus complex is abandoned or repressed by the girl, rather than destroyed, with the result being that the super-ego of the female has less strength than that of males. The resolution of the Oedipus complex for both boys and girls involves the repudiation of femininity, which Freud regarded as bedrock.

Female Homosexuality

Freud's only formulation about female homosexuality is presented in a case study (Freud, 1920) of a young woman who had been sent to see him by her parents, who were deeply concerned about her relationship with an older woman, who they deemed of 'bad character'. Important to note that Freud writes about his initial misgivings about taking the case, stating that he found the girl to have no illness or "neurotic conflict" (p. 150). He also stated that he regarded homosexuality as something that could not be easily changed, further implying that it should not be attempted (p. 151). Freud nevertheless agreed to see her, and did so for a short period of time.

In this case study, Freud described the young woman as displaying what he regarded as a "masculine attitude" towards a feminine love-object (1920, p. 154). In exploring her childhood history, he observed her to have passed through the 'normal' stages of the Oedipus complex for girls, at first turning to her father and then an older brother as object of desire, later developing a "maternal attitude" in early adolescence (p. 156). Freud observed that things changed when her mother gave birth to a third boy, when the patient was 16. Freud suggested that the older woman whom the patient had fallen in love with was a substitute for her mother. However, the woman's manner also reminded the patient of her older brother. Freud states:

> Her lady's slender figure, severe beauty, and downright manner reminded her of the brother who was a little older than herself. Her latest choice corresponded, therefore, not only to her feminine but also to her masculine ideal; it combined satisfaction of the homosexual tendency with that of the heterosexual one.
>
> (1920, pp. 156–157)

Here Freud refers to innate bisexuality in his understanding of this young woman's object choice. Freud came to understand that, as the girl was "experiencing the revival of her infantile

Oedipus complex at puberty" (p. 157), she suffered a disappointment towards her mother, who was perceived as favouring male children. The patient was angry at the mother bearing the child that she had unconsciously wished for from her father. Furious with her father for such betrayal, she turned away from him and from men and repudiated her wish to have a child of her own. The patient, observing her father's anger at her relationship with the other woman, also regarded this as a means to take her revenge on him.

Interesting to note that in this case study, Freud suggested that the young woman's mother, perceiving her more youthful, beautiful daughter as a competitor, kept a possessive hold over her daughter, getting in the way of her developing a close relationship with her father (p. 157). Here Freud suggests the influential role of the parent's own sexuality and fantasies, rather than focusing entirely on internal drives. The influence of the parent's sexuality on a child's developing sexuality is developed further by several later theorists, discussed in other chapters of the book.

In his later writing on female sexuality, Freud (1931) pointed out that the girl's Oedipal development begins with a 'negative' Oedipus complex, in that the girl has her mother as first object of desire. She only reaches a 'positive' Oedipus complex by "surmounting" the period of the 'negative' complex (p. 226). He partly explains this in terms of the girl's innate bisexuality, and with the conceptualisation of the little girl as at first adopting a masculine character (as discussed above). Thus, according to him, the girl 'changes' her own sex as well as changes the sex of her object (p. 228). However, in "defiant self-assertiveness to her threatened masculinity" (p. 229) the girl may retain her masculine character and develop a homosexual orientation. The notion of a 'primary femininity' is taken up by later theorists (discussed mostly in Chapter 4).

Psychic Bisexuality and the Complete Oedipus Complex

From early on in his writing, Freud (1905) regarded bisexuality as an innate aspect of human sexuality. In *The Ego and the Id*, Freud (1923) expanded on his notion of psychic bisexuality to introduce the concept of the 'complete Oedipus complex', which provided a more nuanced understanding of sexuality, involving the presence of both the 'positive' and 'negative' Oedipus complex in the sexuality of every individual. For example, he writes:

> Closer study usually discloses the more complete Oedipus complex, which is twofold, positive and negative, and is due to the bisexuality originally present in children; that is to say that a boy has not merely an ambivalent attitude towards his father, and an affectionate object choice towards his mother, but at the same time he also behaves like a girl and displays an affectionate feminine attitude to his father and a corresponding jealousy and hostility towards his mother.
>
> (1923, p. 33)

Freud's conceptualisation of psychic bisexuality seemed to mostly retain a heterosexual framework. For example, when referring to the boy's bisexuality and the complete Oedipus complex, Freud (1925) describes the boy's desire to be the love-object of his father as his adoption of a 'feminine' attitude. In his case study of a young homosexual woman (Freud, 1920), he described her as adopting a 'masculine' attitude. As Judith Butler (1990) points out:

> The conceptualization of bisexuality in terms of *dispositions*, feminine and masculine, which have heterosexual aims as their intentional correlates, suggests that for Freud *bisexuality is the coincidence of two heterosexual desires within a single psyche.* The masculine disposition is, in effect, never oriented toward the father as an object of sexual love, and neither is the feminine disposition oriented towards the mother. ... Hence, within Freud's thesis of primary bisexuality, there is no homosexuality, and only opposites attract.
>
> (p. 82)

However, in some places he seems to describe the possibility of sexuality and gender identifications that were more mixed and fluid; for example, in the *Three Essays*, he writes:

in human beings pure masculinity or femininity is not to be found either in a psychological or a biological sense. Every individual on the contrary displays a mixture of the character-traits belonging to his own and to the opposite sex; and he shows a combination of activity and passivity whether or not these last character-traits tally with his biological ones.

(Freud, 1905; footnote on p. 219)

Contemporary psychoanalytic theorists (e.g. Heenen-Wolff, 2011; Luepnitz, 2019, 2021), suggest that Freud's notion of innate bisexuality and the complete Oedipus complex can be read in less heteronormative terms, and that focusing on this aspect of Freud's work is crucial for a more nuanced understanding of homo-sexuality and bisexuality, as well as heterosexuality. This will be discussed further in Chapter 7.

Some Key Points of Critique

There have been numerous critiques made over the years of Freud's theory of sexuality, and how he conceptualised the Oedi-pus complex. Some of these will be outlined in later chapters, but I will flag up some key points here. It is important, I think, to recognise that Freud was writing in a far more conservative era than today. We may find some of his writing expresses some con-servative or problematic attitudes, but at the time he was writing, he was considered by many to be 'dangerous' because of his views on sexuality being so liberal.

Feminist psychoanalysts and social theorists have critiqued the centrality of the penis, the phallic, in Freud's theory and the notion of penis envy and castration anxiety as the basis for understanding female sexuality and identity development. Female sexuality is cast in the negative. As the French psychoanalyst, Janine Chasseguet-Smirgel (1976), summarises:

Female sexuality is therefore a series of lacks: the lack of a vagina, lack of a penis, lack of a specific sexuality, lack of an adequate erotic object, and finally the lacks which are implied by her being devoid of any intrinsic feminine qualities which she could cathect directly and by her being forced to give up the clitoris. We can add the relative lack of a superego and the capacity for sublimation, issues which I shall not be able to discuss here. The boy's sexuality is so much more full: he possesses an adequate sexual organ, a sexuality which is specific from the outset, and two love-objects to satisfy the requirements of both tendencies of the Oedipus complex.

(p. 281)

While he did acknowledge his difficulty and struggle in trying to understand female sexuality (e.g. Freud, 1931), his writing on female sexuality was problematic to say the least. Critiques of penis envy and castration anxiety, and feminist revisions of female sexuality and the female Oedipus complex, are explored mostly in Chapters 4 and 6.

Another critique made of Freud's theory of the Oedipus complex is that it centres entirely on the desires and wishes of the child and does not consider adequately the influential role of the parent. This is explored further in Chapter 5 when looking at perspectives from French psychoanalysis and in particular the work of Jean Laplanche and the enigmatic aspects of sexuality. This is also challenged in relational perspectives, discussed in Chapter 6.

As stated earlier, while Freud did not explicitly regard homosexuality as pathology, his formulations of the 'negative' Oedipus complex is nevertheless problematic at times, as it suggests an 'arrest' in what he regarded as 'normal' development and often tends to adopt a heteronormative organising framework. Some non-pathologising reformulations of homosexuality are explored in Chapter 7.

Chapter 3

Klein and the Oedipal Situation

Melanie Klein made an important development, and departure, from Freud's theories, placing far greater emphasis on the first year of life of the infant. She regarded the Oedipus complex as an important stage of development, but considered how early stages of it exist from the start of life, with the infant being born into an Oedipal *situation*. In this chapter I outline Klein's ideas about the Oedipal situation as it is linked to her concepts of the paranoid-schizoid and depressive positions. I will then discuss her concept of the 'combined parent figure' in the Oedipus situation. Following this, I will outline some important contributions made by contemporary Kleinian psychoanalysts. Finally, I will introduce some moves towards more relational psychoanalytic approaches that develop from Klein's work (which link to some of the theories discussed in Chapter 6).

The Oedipal Situation

Klein (1928) observed how children's phantasies that reflect Oedipal dynamics could be interpreted symbolically in the play of children as young as one. She further regarded these symbolised Oedipal dynamics as a continuation of the much earlier intense anxieties of the oral stage of psychosexual development. Klein viewed the infant as being born into an Oedipal *situation*, where the anxieties and dynamics of the Oedipus complex itself (as it develops later in infancy) are embedded within the infant's earliest interactions with their primary caregivers. The content of these

DOI: 10.4324/9781003394471-3

anxieties arises from unconscious phantasies that the child has about their primary objects (mother and father). Klein used the term phantasies with a 'ph' to distinguish it from 'fantasy' (a genre of story-telling). Freud suggested that a child's Oedipal phantasies only emerge in the phallic stage of development. For Klein, such Oedipal phantasies exist in the unconscious from the start, in rudimentary form.

Klein (1932) focused on the development of an inner world (psychic reality) as distinct from the external world; an inner world of unconscious mental representations, or unconscious phantasies, based on the child's subjective experience of their external world, and their bodily sensations. For Klein, unconscious phantasies are the mental representations of instincts. In turn, these unconscious phantasies colour or distort our experience of external reality. Klein understood our capacity for phantasy to be innate, in that we are born with some innate prototypical knowledge, which includes prototypical knowledge about the penis and the vagina, and about sex or the 'primal scene'. That is, the infant has a rudimentary innate awareness of the parental couple and the parent's sexuality, both in phantasy and in perception of the mother and father (Klein, 1928). Here, Klein challenged Freud's suggestion that the girl (and boy) has no knowledge of the vagina until puberty, a challenge also made by Karen Horney and others (see Chapter 4).

Klein regarded the infant's early relationship to the mother, and subsequently the father, in the first year of life as important early stages of the Oedipus complex for both males and females. These early relationships to the primary objects are experienced in terms of the child's libidinal and aggressive impulses towards the mother and father. While Freud emphasised the role of desire and rivalry in the Oedipus complex, Klein focused on the powerful emotions of love, envy, and hatred that manifest much earlier in a child's life. Klein's understanding of the Oedipus complex and its resolution are tied deeply to her concepts of the paranoid-schizoid and depressive positions. For readers less familiar with Klein, I will provide a brief outline of the two positions.

The Paranoid-Schizoid and the Depressive Positions

One of Klein's (1932, 1935, 1946, 1959) most important theoretical contributions was her formulation of the paranoid-schizoid position and the depressive position, occurring primarily during the first year of life. Her use of the term 'position' describes these two as fluctuating and overlapping mental states, rather than fixed developmental 'stages'. Although she describes these two positions of early life, they continue to exist in some form as fluctuating mental states into adulthood.

Klein argued that the early experience of the infant involves intense anxiety arising out of their aggressive instinct, as well as their absolute dependence on the mother as primary caregiver. Klein placed greater emphasis on the aggressive instinct than the sexual instinct. In the paranoid-schizoid position (around the first six months of life), the infant has a rudimentary ego, and developmentally, the infant is not yet able to perceive and experience the mother as a whole, separate object. Its experience of the mother is that of a relationship to part-objects, most significantly, a part-object relationship to the mother's breast during feeding. The infant has a split experience of the mother, as involving a relationship with a 'good' breast/mother when the infant is nurtured and fed, and a separate 'bad' breast/mother when the infant is frustrated and hungry. The infant utilises omnipotent defences of splitting and projection to attempt to rid itself of destructive, persecutory sensations, and to retain the presence of 'good' sensations. With the 'good' breast, the infant has an ideal experience. The infant incorporates the feelings of goodness and nurturance of the mother as if it were their own; the infant has a good experience of self, with the mother experienced in turn as 'good'. Alternatively, 'bad' internal feelings (e.g. hunger pains, aggression) are to be gotten rid of. These 'bad' feelings are projected onto the breast/mother, who is then perceived as the 'bad', withholding object. The infant also utilises the omnipotent defence of hallucinating the presence of the breast, for example the thumb in the mouth hallucinated as the nipple in the mouth, providing the illusion that the 'good' breast is in their possession and under their control.

However, the attempts to possess the 'good' and get rid of the 'bad' ultimately do not work, as the breast inevitably cannot always be present, and hunger pains always return. The absence of the 'good' breast evokes powerful feelings of loss and abandonment in the infant. The infant forms a polarised experience of the mother, with strong libidinal feelings towards the 'good' breast/ mother which it loves and wishes to possess, and conflicting aggressive feelings towards the 'bad' breast/mother which it hates. Chasseguet-Smirgel (1988) later suggested that in the paranoid-schizoid position there is the following triangular arrangement: the child, the good or ideal object, and the bad or persecutory object. She suggests this to be an archaic matrix of the Oedipus complex.

Klein also understood there to be, from a very early age, a wish, or a drive to know about, get inside and to take over or destroy the mother's body. There is an awareness of and envy for the mother's goodness. Such expressions of envy and hatred can be observed in the infant at times biting the mother's nipple, for example. As the child moves into the depressive position, they come to fear that the mother will retaliate for the attacks made on her body. Chasseguet-Smirgel (1989) later posited that behind the phantasies of emptying the mother's body of all that exists inside lies a more archaic wish or desire to return to the mother's womb. As a result of this archaic wish, the infant wishes to destroy all obstacles that get in the way of its return to the mother's womb, including the father's penis.

In the depressive position (from around 6 months), the infant's cognitive and emotional capacities evolve, and they start perceiving the mother as a whole, separate person. With this comes the realisation that the mother is both the 'good' breast/mother and the 'bad' breast/mother. In the depressive position, the child starts to acknowledge the mother's separateness, complexity, and feelings, leading to the integration of the 'good' and 'bad' mother and the child's own 'good' and 'bad' experiences and feelings. The child comes to understand that its feelings of love and hate are directed at the same person. When the breast is absent there is the phantasy that the child has eaten up the breast out of greed and destroyed it. This is accompanied by feelings of guilt and anxiety over the harm done to the object in phantasy, and the fears of losing the 'good object'. There is also the experience of loss of the omnipotent phantasies of possessing the 'good', idealised breast, and having to mourn its loss. This is most salient at the point of weaning. This sense of loss and mourning the ideal which cannot be had, and objects that cannot be controlled, are the fundamental experience of the depressive position for the child, and on through adulthood. The realisation that the 'bad' object is also the 'good' object leads to a wish to repair and restore the loved object. Such attempts at reparation can be observed through the child's play or gestures that demonstrate love and care. For Freud, the development of the superego was one of the outcomes of the resolution of the Oedipus complex. For Klein, the superego exists at an earlier age, observed by the guilt anxieties experienced by the child.

The Combined Parent Figure

Freud (1918) made reference to the concept of the primal scene and observed that the young child has phantasies related to the primal scene, but he didn't incorporate these features much as an important part of the Oedipus complex. For Klein, phantasies about the primal scene formed a fundamental component of the Oedipus situation. In early infancy, these phantasies are imbued with aggressive and sadistic ideas. Phantasies about the primal scene and the perception and experience of the parental couple changes in the shift from the paranoid-schizoid position into the depressive position, and into the Oedipus complex proper.

The commencement of the Oedipus complex at the early stage of infancy coincides with the child's 'polymorphously perverse' instinctual impulses described by Freud. As a result, the child is in a constant state of instinctual fluctuation and conflict as excitation is located in all areas of the body and with all objects. Unconscious phantasies of the breast, penis, faeces, child, as well as the primal scene and the parental couple, are all mixed up. Klein regarded the infant as preoccupied with the parental couple from an early age and formulated the concept of the 'combined parental figure', a terrifying phantasy figure of the mother's body incorporating the penis inside it, as well as including rival babies. This combined figure is a very early, rudimentary conception of the parental couple locked in pleasure. It evokes envy and sadistic aggression in the infant, as well as fear of retribution, and thus is terrifying. This combined parent figure is often symbolised by children in the form of monsters, for example 'the monster in the cupboard'. Klein describes it as such:

> The child expects to find within the mother a) the father's penis, b) the excrement, and c) the children, and these things it equates with edible substances. According to the child's earliest phantasies (or 'sexual theories') of parental coitus, the father's penis (or his whole body) becomes incorporated in the mother during the act. Thus the child's sadistic attacks have for their object both father and mother, who are in phantasy bitten, torn, cut or stamped to bits. The attacks give rise to anxiety lest the subject should be punished by the united parents, and this anxiety also becomes internalised in consequence of the oral-sadistic introjection of the objects and is thus already directed towards the early super-ego.
>
> (1930, p. 219)

The combined parent figure can often be symbolised in horror movies. For example, Glen Gabbard and Krin Gabbard (1999) offer a Kleinian analysis of Ridley Scott's 1979 film, *Alien*. The film is full of horror imagery that symbolises the intense persecutory anxieties of the paranoid-schizoid position. In the film there is the constant persecutory presence of the malevolent 'Mother'. Gabbard and Gabbard suggest that there is a frightening combined parent couple depicted by the android Ash (a father figure) working under the control of 'Mother' – the penis inside the mother. The alien monster is a terrifying combined parent figure, phallic-like, with an inner set of teeth. The movie depicts the crew's exploration of the interior of an abandoned ship, which is "womblike" and contains egglike shapes in its depth (p. 284). This is reminiscent of the child's paranoid-schizoid phantasies of wanting to get inside the interior of the mother's body and extract the babies within.

As mentioned earlier, Klein suggested that for both the girl and the boy, there is an inherent unconscious knowledge of the vagina as well as the penis. The model of the nipple in the mouth of the oral period has an equivalent model of the penis in the vagina in phantasy. During the oral period, both the girl and the boy shift in their oral desire for the nipple to the father's penis as nipple in phantasy. The penis becomes a substitute for the breast, both of which are experienced in part-object form. We are not talking about the *actual* penis here, Klein is referring to an unconscious mental representation of an object (father), at this stage a part-object. This desire for the penis as nipple is the early stages of the girl's 'positive' (heteroerotic) and the boy's 'negative' (homoerotic) Oedipus complex. The father's penis too comes to be represented as 'good' and 'bad' in phantasy. Attempts may be made to keep the parental couple separate and keep an omnipotent relationship to each of them. Klein regarded both the positive and negative Oedipus complex to exist simultaneously and for libidinal and aggressive impulses to shift from one parental object to the other. She states:

> Each object, therefore, is in turn liable to become at times good, at times bad. This movement to and fro between various aspects of the primary imagos implies a close interaction between the early stages of the inverted and positive Oedipus complex.
>
> (Klein, 1945, p. 409)

According to Klein, the depressive position marks the beginning of the Oedipus complex proper, as the focus of the child's attention centres on the parental couple, and the gradual acceptance of the parental couple as separate to the child. As the child moves to the depressive position, the combined parent figure becomes the parental couple; two separate individual figures that come together in a relationship. Anxieties in relation to these separate, whole objects now involve jealousy, feelings of exclusion, and loss of omnipotence. For Klein, the Oedipal feelings of love, rivalry, and envy aren't just directed at the opposite-sex parent, they are also strongly felt towards the same-sex parent. The mother is both the desired and the envied object, and the father plays a dual role as a rival and a protective figure against the child's own aggressive impulses towards the mother. As the child progresses through the depressive position, and there is a growing recognition of reality, they gradually develop a more integrated and empathetic view of their parents. This allows them to navigate the Oedipal conflicts with a deeper understanding of the consequences of their desires and actions, and how they might come into conflict with the desires of others, particularly their parents.

Klein's resolution of the Oedipus complex, and working through of the depressive position, involves mourning the unattainable primary object, coming to terms with the loss, and moving on to subsequent developmental milestones. While Klein observed the existence of both the 'positive' and 'negative' Oedipus complex in both girls and boys, she regarded heterosexual object choice as the optimal resolution of the Oedipus complex, viewing homosexual object choice as occurring out of a defensive turning away against retaliation from the opposite sex parent. This is a formulation that has been critiqued for ignoring any form of positive same-sex desire (O'Connor & Ryan, 1993).

An Emphasis on Love and Hate

Ruth Stein (1990) in a proposed rereading of some of Klein's work suggested we might approach some of Klein's concepts in terms of what it says about affects and their functioning; what she refers to as Klein's "theory of feelings" (p. 500). As she points out, Klein moved from Freud's explanation of instinctual impulses being cathected onto objects, to her articulation of the loving and hateful feelings experienced in relation to an object, and the conflict of feelings one has towards one's external and internal objects throughout life. It is feelings too that create internal objects ('good' or 'bad'). As Stein describes it:

> Objects, according to Klein, possess from the beginning psychological features in the infant's eyes and stir up many feelings in him. The object is not only an instinctually gratifying or frustrating object, but a loving and loved, or a hating and hated, or envious or envied, object.
>
> (p. 504)

Stein points out how Klein seemed to focus on the process of how the child (and later, the adult) attempts to regulate unbearable feelings. These conflicting feelings are managed in differing ways in the paranoid-schizoid position and the depressive position. In terms of the Oedipus complex, the emphasis is on the management of conflicting feelings of love and hate towards objects, conflicting feelings which arouse anxiety and guilt. As a result of this, during the stage of the Oedipus complex, these anxieties are managed by attaching more feelings of love, desire, and need for reparation to one object (e.g. the mother) and attaching feelings of anxiety and hate to the other object (e.g. the father) (p. 505).

Contemporary Kleinian Developments in Relation to the Oedipus Complex

Among the contemporary Kleinian psychoanalysts, two in particular have made important contributions to Klein's theoretical development of the Oedipal situation and Oedipus complex: Ronald Britton and John Steiner.

Britton (1989) expanded on Klein's conception of the combined parent figure and relationship to the parental couple in the Oedipal situation, to conceptualise the Oedipal situation as involving a triangulated relationship. In the depressive position, the child comes to learn that they cannot solely possess the mother or the father, as the rivalrous parent stands in the way. This loss may be experienced as persecutory, if it cannot be tolerated. The child also comes to learn that the parental couple have a sexual, genital relationship, which the child–parent relationship is not. The child is thus excluded from the parental relationship. Each parent also has a distinct relationship to their child that differs from the relationship that the other parent has. Thus, where there are heterosexual parents, there is a child–mother relationship, a child–father relationship and a mother–father relationship.

According to Britton, the depressive position is worked through when the child comes to accept the reality of the parental couple relationship, hopefully a loving and creative couple relationship, which in turn is internalised. It is an external and internalised parental couple relationship that the child can be an observer of as well as have a relationship to. This creates what Britton calls a "triangular space", which he defines as "a space bounded by the three persons of the Oedipal situation and all their potential relationships" (1989, p. 86). In this triangular space, the child is able to reflect on themselves and their relationship to others. Britton refers to Bion and his paper "Attacks on linking" (1959) to understand how for some individuals, the reality of parental sexuality (their sexual link) is perceived as too threatening and potentially catastrophic, as it severs the link to their dyadic relationship to their mother, and so attempts are made to psychically destroy the parental couple link. This then maintains an infantile psychic state that involves the perceived existence of the ideal, 'good' breast and a persecutory world of split-off 'bad' objects.

In the working through of the depressive position and the Oedipus complex, the omnipotent desire to possess one parent must be relinquished as the reality of the parental couple is observed. How the child perceives and reacts to the reality of the Oedipal situation, the parental couple, and what Money-Kyrle (1971) refers to as the 'facts of life',[1] determines their ability to think, to symbolise, and to use their mind in a creative and reflective way (Rusbridger, 2004). Steiner (1985, 1990) suggested that in some cases individuals may 'turn a blind eye' to some of these Oedipal realities. This is different to an attempt to attack any recognition or acknowledgement of reality, as Britton describes with reference to Bion. In 'turning a blind eye' the individual is aware of reality and has a respect for it. But, fearing reality, they choose to misrepresent or distort it, turning to illusions of omnipotence in order to maintain a state of psychic equilibrium, and not be disturbed by the mourning and guilt associated with working through the Oedipus complex and depressive position. Steiner examines the myth of Oedipus and is persuasive in suggesting that Oedipus, and Jocasta, must have at some level known or suspected that Oedipus had indeed killed King Laius and married his widow, and had known the truth of their incestuous relationship. However, they seemed to ignore some obvious facts pointing to this (e.g. Oedipus's scarred ankles and his unclear origin story).

Freud's formulation of the Oedipus complex rests on the assumption that the object of the mother and the object of the father are perceived as separate, whole objects. While Freud described the desire towards the opposite-sex parents and rivalry towards the same-sex parent, he did not formulate this in terms of the child's experience of being excluded from the relationship of the parental couple. As mentioned earlier, Freud writes about the 'primal scene' but does not explicitly link it to the Oedipus complex. For Klein, the child's phantasies about the parental couple are a fundamentally important part of the Oedipus complex. For Britton, the capacity to internalise a creative, observing parental couple is important for the capacity for reflection of self and other in a relationship.

Britton suggests that the depressive position and the Oedipus situation is "never finished" (1992, p. 38), requiring renewed working-through with new life situations and developmental stages. Although Klein described the paranoid-schizoid position and the depressive position consequentially, there is always some oscillation between the two. With regards the Oedipus situation, this oscillation is paralleled by the oscillation between an intolerance of a triangular relationship and an acceptance of it (Rusbridger, 2004). The goal is for there to be a greater move towards integration and the acceptance of reality and triangular space, which are markers of the depressive position.

One possible outcome of an Oedipal situation when it has not been worked through is a sense of resentment and grievance (Steiner, 1996). Here, the intrusion of the third object (father) provokes a strong sense of revenge for harming the narcissistic mother–child dyadic object relationship. This intrusion is perceived as injurious to self and to the idealised good object, and the child feels he must defend self and the idealised good object against this injustice. This situation involves imagined injustice, rather than the experience of actual trauma. Steiner (2018) distinguishes between the trauma of disillusionment brought on by the knowledge of reality in the Oedipal situation, versus actual abusive traumas. In the case of specific abuse, such trauma is the 'truth' and reality that must be faced in the Oedipal situation, rather than the loss of the idealised experience of the infant at the good breast. The reality that needs to be faced is that actual bad and damaging objects do indeed exist. Steiner reminds us of the actual physical and emotional trauma suffered by Oedipus in the myth. In such cases the external impingements need to be considered, but this does not preclude the exploration of unconscious phantasies that nevertheless play a role. For example, Steiner refers to how guilt may exist in the unconscious phantasies of the abuse victim, and not just something to be ascribed to the perpetrator, as difficult as that may be.

Steiner (1999) describes the struggle for dominance that is involved in the resolution of the Oedipus complex, as the child battles to overcome feelings of powerlessness against the perceived power and authority of the parental couple, and the requirement to 'submit' to their authority. He delineates two possible outcomes of the Oedipus situation. One is the paranoid solution involving a retreat from the painful realities of the Oedipus situation and the parental couple, involving the presence of feelings of hatred, revenge, and the resort to the phantasy of omnipotence. The second is the depressive solution, where the realities of the parental couple and the Oedipal situation can be acknowledged and hatred and resentment can be let go of. Feelings of love can emerge, but with this comes feelings of guilt for the previous hatred and damage caused (in phantasy). This is resolved and worked through with developing greater tolerance for these feelings of guilt and loss. Steiner describes the depressive solution as achievable if the child can be developmentally supported in tolerating feelings of guilt and loss, and so he seems to imply the importance of the actual supportive role of the parents here (something that Freud and Klein do not explicitly do). Steiner suggested that these two solutions to the Oedipus complex co-exist and the individual oscillates between one and the other in the same way that an individual can oscillate between the paranoid-schizoid position and the depressive position.

A Move Towards a More Relational Model

Klein's formulation of the depressive position and the Oedipal situation, and in particular Britton's further developments on the triangular dynamics of the Oedipus situation, has been influential for some of the contemporary relational psychoanalytic theorists. One such theorist, Lewis Aron (1995), has contributed to a relational understanding of the internalised primal scene. I introduce Aron's work in this chapter as a way to bridge to some of the developments made by relational psychoanalysts, discussed in Chapter 6.

Aron uses Klein's conception of the combined parental figure and the internalised primal scene as metaphors to illustrate the psychic capacity for the individual to "hold two contrasting ideas in mind simultaneously" in a manner that tolerates ambiguity and facilitates the capacity to symbolise and to think creatively (p. 197). He defines the primal scene as more than just the child's knowledge of, or actual witnessing of, their parent's sexual intercourse, and involves the child's total experience, understanding, and witnessing of their parent's relationship, often symbolised by the phantasy of them in sexual intimacy. He regards the primal scene as the Oedipal drama, in that it involves three people: the child, the mother, and the father and the relationships between them (p. 207). In the shift to the depressive position, the mother and father become disentangled from the combined parent figure to be perceived as separate, whole objects. It is now that they can interact with one another in the primal scene; two separate objects coming together in sexual intercourse.

Aron argues that the transformed internalised parental couple of the depressive position does not replace the frightening internal combined parent figure of the paranoid-schizoid position; the two continue to exist and "to operate synchronically as crucial dimensions of experience" (p. 212), with an oscillation back and forth between the two. This is the basis of his suggestion of the presence of both a unitary sense of self and a multiplicity of self. Drawing on the work of Britton, Aron considers the internalisation of the primal scene and the triangular space that develops as a result as the basis of the development of intersubjectivity as there is an integration of the self as both a subject and an object, and the other as both a subject and an object (p. 217). That is, in the triangular space of the primal scene, the parents are the objects of the child's desires, but the child is also an object excluded from their parents' subjectivity and their intimate relationship. According to Aron, the establishment of subjectivity and the development of intersubjectivity evolves with Oedipal development and the transformation of the combined parent figure to the primal scene. He states:

> a person needs to develop a cohesive sense of self as a subjective-self, a separate centre of subjectivity; of a self-as-agent, an experiencing ego. And the person needs to be aware of, and be able to reflect on, himself or herself as an object of his or her own investigation and of himself or herself as an object of the wishes and intentions of others. These dimensions of self need to be integrated and yet multiple; there should be a sense of both identity and multiplicity.
>
> (Aron, 1995, p. 218)

Although the primal scene is a model of heterosexuality, Aron stresses that this does not preclude an equal consideration of homosexuality. Klein's combined parent figure encompasses both heterosexual and homosexual combinations, as the child is not yet able to distinguish the father, as being a man and having a penis, from the mother, as being a woman and having a vagina, and the transformed combined parent figure can refer to diverse desires, and not only as a model of heterosexual procreation.

Note

1 Money-Kyrle (1971) referred to three key 'facts of life': The infant's dependence on the mother for survival, the acknowledgment of the parent's sexual relationship which the child is excluded from, and aging and the inevitability of death.

Chapter 4

Feminist Critiques of the Oedipus Complex

As some readers will have felt reading Freud, some of his views about female sexuality and the 'female' Oedipus complex are problematic, primarily his emphasis on the phallic, and castration anxiety and penis envy as central. In this chapter I introduce some of the important revisions made to the understanding of female sexuality and the 'female' Oedipus complex, made by mostly female psychoanalysts. I start by presenting some of the critiques made about the concepts of castration anxiety and penis envy in the 'female' Oedipus complex, as well as some revised perspectives on gender differentiation. I will then introduce some different proposed reformulations of the Oedipus complex that claim to provide a more nuanced model for understanding female sexuality. It is important to note that 'feminist' perspectives are not only presented in this chapter. For example, other important psychoanalytic writers that have contributed to a greater understanding of female subjectivity and sexuality, such as Nancy Chodorow and Jessica Benjamin, are discussed in Chapter 6.

Critiques of Castration Anxiety and Penis Envy

As outlined in Chapter 2, Freud suggested that the female child, not yet aware of her vagina, regards herself as a 'little man' and perceives herself as lacking a penis, and as thus already castrated. Her Oedipus complex is propelled by this castration anxiety and her penis envy. Many psychoanalysts at the time, such as Helene Deutsch and Ernest Jones, challenged this view, bringing to the

DOI: 10.4324/9781003394471-4

fore a more detailed exploration of femininity and female sexuality. One such important figure was Karen Horney.

Similar to other writers at the time, Horney (1924, 1926, 1932, 1933) critiques the masculine-centred perspective of the Oedipus complex and psychosexual development, and provides a challenge to the centrality of penis envy in female development. While acknowledging that some girls may express an envious desire for a penis, she disputed the notion that this 'penis envy' represents a primary, biologically determined phenomenon that drives female development. Horney suggests that the experience of castration anxiety differs for women and men. While both sexes experience a pull towards the parent of the opposite sex and rivalry with the same-sex parent, their anxiety responses to the inevitable barriers to fulfilling these desires differ.

In writing about the observation of a 'castration complex' in women, Horney (1924, 1932) argues that it is not solely rooted in penis envy and the perception of self as castrated, as formulated by Freud, but rather as arising out of frustrations around her own female sexuality and from a repressed phantasy of castration through sexual union with the father. Horney (1924) regarded expressions of penis envy in females as resulting from the girl's observation of a difference afforded to the sexual permissiveness of boys and a perceived sexual disadvantage experienced by girls. Horney observes that boys can easily see their genitals and self-examine them, while girls cannot as easily. This allows boys to develop a sense of superiority, while girls might feel disadvantaged and inferior. Horney also argued that girls were socially required to supress their masturbatory wishes and impulses. She argued that observing that boys can touch their genitals while urinating might lead girls to unconsciously associate urination with masturbation. This could create a sense of injustice for girls who are discouraged from touching themselves. Thus, penis envy is not an envy for the penis itself, but rather the perceived greater power and freedom associated with it.

Furthermore, Horney (1926, 1932) challenges Freud's assertion that the vagina remains 'undiscovered' during childhood, until puberty when the onset of menstruation gives the girl an awareness of the role of her vagina. Drawing on her clinical observations,

Horney argues that the vagina plays an active role in female sexuality from early childhood. Similarly to Klein, Horney suggested that girls (and boys) have an awareness of the vagina from an early age, adding that they have an instinctive understanding of vaginal penetration, arising out of an awareness of the anatomical differences between the sexes.

Horney posited that during the Oedipus complex, when the girl's desires for her father are inevitably frustrated, there does not only occur a renunciation of the father as a love object, but there is also a "flight from womanhood" (1926, p. 333). The forbidden nature of her desire for her father is in part fuelled by an anxiety around the perceived vulnerability of her female genitals, and the social roles of women. Horney suggests there is also a deeply repressed phantasy of having been castrated through a sexual act with the father. According to Horney, the girl is aware of the size difference between her and her father, and thus of the size difference between her vagina and her father's penis. This results in a deep-seated fear of penetration and injury, even destruction of her genitals, which is then heightened by observing or learning about the menstruation of women and physical traumas of miscarriage or childbirth. This fear is amplified by the girl's inability to verify the intactness of her genitals, unlike the boy who can visually inspect his penis (Horney, 1933).

Another factor contributing to the 'flight from womanhood' are the girl's feelings of guilt and insecurity about the female body, which Horney argues are formed through societal and cultural messages about female inferiority, negative experiences associated with masturbation, and the perceived vulnerability associated with menstruation. According to Horney (1926), in order to cope with this anxiety and guilt, the girl identifies with the father and adopts a 'masculine attitude', adopting a "fictitious male role" (p. 335) as a defence against the anxiety and guilt associated with her Oedipal desires. She attempts to repress her feminine desires and deny the significance of her own genitals. This provides her with a temporary escape but ultimately leads to feelings of inadequacy and a distorted self-image. The historical subordination of women and the pervasive societal messages about female inferiority create a reality where embracing femininity can feel disempowering and disadvantageous. The girl regresses to the pre-Oedipal stage of penis envy, intensifying the desire for the penis as a symbol of power and a means of escaping her perceived inferiority. Horney, therefore, viewed penis envy in girls as secondary rather than primary.

Regarding the boy's experience, Horney (1932, 1933) suggests that boys do not just have an awareness of having a penis and others not, but also have an awareness of the vagina and an understanding and a desire to penetrate. She argues that the boy, encountering the impossible nature of his desire for his mother, experiences a narcissistic wound to his sense of masculinity. This is exacerbated by the perceived size difference between his own genitals and his mother's, leading to feelings of inadequacy and the fear of rejection and ridicule. Horney suggests that the boy copes with his narcissistic wound by repressing his desire for his mother and reinforcing his phallic narcissism, withdrawing into himself and denying the significance of the female genital, which is also feared. This, according to Horney, is the basis of the phallic phase described by Freud, where the boy's focus shifts to his own penis and a desire to prove its potency. The boy's anxiety primarily revolves around his self-respect and masculinity, leading to a need to constantly assert his potency and dominance over women. A dread of motherhood and of the vagina also develops, becoming "an object of castration anxiety" (Horney, 1932, p. 357) – for example as symbolised by the *vagina dentata*. This stems from the fact that it is often the mother that first prohibits the instinctual activities of the male child, which stimulates rage and hostility towards the mother's body. A fear of the vagina can manifest in hostility and a sadistic attitude towards the mother and towards women, who are then objectified and denigrated. Horney (1932) seemed to regard male homosexuality as only to be explained by a fear and dread of the vagina that is then turned away from in disgust.

Horney (1926, 1933) also observed the existence of male envy towards female sexuality. As a counter to the idea that only the female envies the male genital, she argues that males experience unconscious envy of motherhood, and the female's biological capability to be pregnant and have children, that they have breasts and the ability to breastfeed, all experiences that they feel excluded from. She argued that this envy can fuel a powerful drive towards achievement in men, as a means of compensating for their lack in reproductive capabilities. The envy and anxieties around the perceived power of women and their reproductive capabilities can also be defended against through a need to conquer and control women, and by devaluating motherhood. Thus, rather than the phallic-centric formulations of Freud, Horney suggested that each sex experiences envy of the opposite sex and their bodies.

Essentially, Horney argues that the boy's Oedipal journey is rooted in his sense of inadequacy and fear of rejection and humiliation, leading him to overemphasise his masculinity. The girl's anxiety about the vulnerability of her body and fear of penetration and injury leads her to partly reject her femininity. This fundamental difference, she contends, shapes their respective psychological development and their often-ambivalent attitudes towards the opposite sex.

The French psychoanalyst, Chasseguet-Smirgel (1976), does not draw much on the work of Horney, yet makes some similar arguments with regards the male's early awareness of the vagina and the narcissistic wound that this inflicts. She re-examines Freud's case study of Little Hans to observe that Hans seemed to have an awareness of the vagina as expressed in his fantasies about wanting to genitally possess his mother, but having a penis that was too little to satisfy her (p. 278). She also points out that if the male child had no apparent knowledge of the vagina and thus had no wish to penetrate the vagina, then, during the Oedipus complex, he would have little reason to envy the father and his bigger penis. Chasseguet-Smirgel (1976) later developed on this idea to argue that reality is not only founded in the observed anatomical differences between the sexes, which includes an early awareness of the vagina, but also the observed differences of the generations: "The reality is not that the mother has been castrated but that she possesses a vagina that the child is utterly unable to (ful)fill" (p. 282). The father possesses the bigger penis that the little boy does not have. The recognition of this reality and the boy's inadequacy in this regard causes a narcissistic wound.

On Primary Femininity

As mentioned earlier, Horney, and others, suggested that there exists a primary awareness of female sexuality in girls. She has an early awareness of her female genitalia and body, which exists before any phase of penis envy. Stoller (1968), in his work on gender identity, later developed the concept of 'primary femininity', based on this early sense and acceptance of femaleness.

Other psychoanalysts such as Elizabeth Mayer (1985) also suggested the existence of a primary femininity, and an early awareness of a vagina, or 'inside space'. Mayer suggests that fantasies about females being genitally open (p. 331) contribute to an anxiety about the capacity for openness and emotional openness being at risk of being lost, as depicted in perceptions of men being emotionally 'closed'. The fantasy being that men have "been closed off genitally" (p. 332). She understands this, in part, as a defensive perception that attributes the idea of lack or 'something missing' to a male, but also to an early fantasy that boys have/had 'open' female genitals like girls, but they have been 'closed off'. Thus, boys fantasise that all children are like them, and have/had a penis, and girls fantasise that all children are like them, and have/had a vagina. For Mayer, castration anxiety, for males and for females, refers to the fear of "losing that genital which is actually possessed" (p. 332), although she acknowledges that castration anxiety for females can also take the form of anxiety about having lost a penis.

Dianne Elise (1997) provides a critique of the notion of 'primary femininity', arguing for a separation of concepts of sex and gender, suggesting that one can talk about the existence of a "primary sense of femaleness" (p. 494), with the girl aware of her sexed female body, but to be distinguished from the concept of 'femininity', which she argues is not innate nor derived from the body. She stresses the need to separate sex from gender from sexual orientation, which for many decades, many psychoanalysts viewed as having to be aligned when speaking about psychic health. I will return to this in Chapter 7 when discussing the Oedipus complex and contemporary psychoanalytic views on homosexuality.

Other Perspectives on Penis Envy

Juliet Mitchell (1974) offered a different feminist reading of psychoanalysis that did not dismiss Freud's theory of castration anxiety and penis envy, regarding them as important aspects of an explanatory model for the perpetuation of the patriarchal society. She considered Freud's ideas in *Totem and Taboo* of the inherited Oedipus complex (see Chapter 8) and his formulation of the female Oedipus complex, noting that Freud suggested that culture, that is patriarchal culture, is transmitted through the boy's and girl's symbolic submission to the power of castration threat. She critiqued Horney, and her suggestion of a primary femininity (and primary heterosexuality), that suggests that a 'woman' and a 'man' are created in nature, supporting Freud's implication that "a man and woman are *made* in culture" (p. 131; italics in original). She went on to propose that we need to "know the devil you have got", rather than search for a more utopian view. She states: "we have a culture in which, with infinite complexity, the self is created divisively, the sexes are divided divisively; a patriarchal culture in which the phallus is valorized and women oppressed" (p. 361). She thought that Freud, in his formulation of the Oedipus complex, attempted to provide us with an account for patriarchal society and the "condition of women" (p. 362). She concludes:

> Freud's analysis of the psychology of women takes place within a concept that it is neither socially nor biologically dualistic. It takes place within an analysis of patriarchy. His theories give us the beginnings of an explanation of the inferiorized and 'alternative' (second sex) psychology of women under patriarchy. Their concern is with how the human animal with a bisexual psychological disposition becomes the sexed social creature – the man or the woman.
>
> (Mitchell, 1974, p. 402)

Another more recent perspective on penis envy comes from Zepf and Seel (2016). They draw on the work of Laplanche and the enigmatic dimension of sexuality (discussed in Chapter 5), to offer a reconceptualisation of penis envy and the girl's Oedipus complex, that is linked to her parent's unconscious Oedipal desires, rather than driven by a perception of castration and lack. They propose that the daughter internalises her parent's own projected positive and negative Oedipal strivings into her unconscious and identifies with some of these strivings to prevent the loss of her parents. The daughter's desire to have her "father's penis *in herself*" derives from her parents own positive Oedipal dynamics (p. 414; italics in original). She envies her mother having possession of the father's penis. Fearing her mother's retaliation for her incestuous wishes, the daughter withdraws from her father as an object of desire, at a conscious level, but retaining her incestuous wish at an unconscious level. Identifying with the parent's negative Oedipus complexes, and out of fear of losing her mother's love, the daughter wishes to be equipped with a penis, "to have her father's penis *on herself*" (p. 415; italics in original), in order to satisfy the desires of her mother, and so envying her father's penis. These heterosexual and homosexual currents occur simultaneously. They suggest that such a view does not differ from some of the ideas posed by Freud in some of his writings, where he seemed to acknowledge the influence of the parent's own Oedipal conflicts on the child, and his conceptualisation of the 'complete' Oedipus complex.

The Oedipus Complex and Gender Differentiation

Irene Fast (1978, 1979, 1990) too presents a critique of Freud's theories of gender development, and its phallo-centricity. Like Horney and others, Fast challenges Freud's formulation of girls being initially masculine in their gender orientation and understands that the girl (and boy) has an early awareness of the vagina and thus female sexuality. However, she takes a different perspective on the development of gender in relation to the Oedipus complex.

Developing further Freud's conceptualisation of an innate psychic bisexuality, Fast develops a model of gender *differentiation* in the Oedipus complex. She argues that prior to children's recognition of the anatomical differences between the sexes, children's early gender experiences are undifferentiated and overinclusive.

She describes the existence of a 'bisexual matrix', where little children do not conceptualise their experiences in gendered terms. During this period, they may internalise characteristics of people in their environment, including male and female attributes, without any sense of limitation based on their biological sex. The little child assumes that all people, including themselves, are the same, possessing the potential for both male and female characteristics. This can be observed in children's fantasies of mothers also possessing a penis, and fathers being capable of having a baby (as Little Hans imagined). Fast argues that such fantasies involved a perception of 'bisexual completeness'. According to Fast, the recognition of anatomical sex difference and the beginning of the Oedipus complex marks the beginning of gender differentiation, a process akin to other developmental differentiations, such as the differentiation of self and other, and subjective and objective reality. With the awareness of anatomical sex differences, the child has to relinquish some of their earlier identifications, which is experienced as a loss.

According to Fast, during the stage of the Oedipus complex, girls are not shifting from a masculine identification to a feminine one, but rather are developing a sense of femininity in relation to their understanding of masculinity. For girls, the recognition that boys have a penis while they do not leads to feelings of envy and loss. However, Fast argues that this is not simply a wish to be male, as Freud suggested. Rather, it represents a protest against the recognition of limitation of their female sex, and a longing for the earlier sense of bisexual wholeness and unlimited gender potential. The penis becomes a symbol for this lost potential, not necessarily a desired object in itself. The relationship with the mother is not simply one of hatred and disappointment, and an attachment to her does not presuppose the development of a masculine or homosexual orientation. She emphasised the important role played by the girl's attachment to her mother in terms of identification and a model for feminine development. The desire for a baby from the father incorporates both the identification with the mother's female capacity for childbirth and the development of a heterosexual relationship.

Meanwhile, for boys, Fast suggests that they do not enter the Oedipal period as unequivocally masculine but rather are struggling to relinquish claims to female/feminine attributes. The recognition of the mother's role in childbirth triggers the boy's interest in sex difference and forces him to confront his own limitations, for example the inability to be pregnant and give birth to a baby. For Fast, the castration anxiety of boys becomes more complex, incorporating not only the rivalry-based threat from the father but also the boy's own repudiated desire for female characteristics.

The process of gender differentiation in the Oedipal period is a critical developmental step in which children confront the limits of their own sex and begin to categorise their experiences in gendered terms. Fast understood that both parents had an influential role to play in the child's gender development, not just primarily the father, as Freud suggested. According to Fast, this differentiation process involves several key tasks: relinquishing fantasies, behaviours and traits that are regarded as incongruent with their biological sex, and projecting the attributes they have renounced onto members of the opposite sex, and in so doing solidifying their understanding of gender differences. The process of differentiation also involves understanding that the opposite sex, while possessing certain attributes, also has its own limitations.

Jessica Benjamin (1998) (to be discussed more in Chapter 6), drawing on the work of Fast on bisexual identifications, argues that girls and boys both become more separate from their primary caregiver (most often the mother), but do not disidentify from them. Both girls and boys make use of a second parental or adult figure to support their developing individuation and independence. Thus, in a heterosexual family, "children of both sexes will, during rapprochement, differentiate mother and father as source of goodness and subject of desire respectively" (pp. 60–61).

Considering Alternative Models for the Oedipus Complex

Some writers have offered other alternative models of the Oedipus complex in an attempt to capture a more nuanced understanding of female sexuality. I will outline the ideas offered by Dianne Elise and the proposed *Persephone* complex formulated by Nancy Kulish and Deanna Holtzman.

A Maternal and a Paternal Oedipus Situation

Elise (2000), developing on the idea of innate bisexuality, suggested that we can consider a primary-maternal Oedipal situation, that both boys and girls have with their mother, and a secondary-paternal Oedipal situation, that girls and boys have with their fathers. She suggests that with fathers increasingly becoming more present in early caretaking of infants, we might talk of primary-maternal and primary-paternal Oedipal situations (p. 134).

Elise suggests that for the girl, her primary Oedipal desires towards the mother are thwarted due to societal prohibitions and the mother's own heterosexual desires. The mother turns away from, or even denies, her daughter's homosexual desire towards her. When the mother desires the father/penis, the daughter may experience a sense of rejection and inadequacy, contributing to feelings of being 'less than'. The boy's desire for his mother is at first acknowledged and then forbidden, while the girl's desire is typically erased and rendered invisible.

The secondary Oedipal situation involves the relationship each sex has in desiring the father. This is where significant gender differences emerge. The boy, in identifying with the father and taking the mother as his love object, can to some extent re-enact his primary Oedipal desires in a socially sanctioned way. However, the girl, in turning to the father, faces a second loss stemming from her desires towards her father being forbidden, or from the "absence" of the paternal penis (Elise, 1998). This does not solely refer to the literal presence or absence of the father but might encompass the father's emotional distance or disengagement or a symbolic absence where the mother prioritises the father/penis over the daughter. Elise (1998) argues that the girl's experience of the 'absent' paternal penis can lead to feelings of emptiness, lack, and incompleteness, contributing to a defensive focus on the penis as a symbol of wholeness and fulfilment. She highlights how, for the girl, her Oedipal complex may involve a double disappointment – a loss of both the primary and secondary object of Oedipal desire. As a result, Elise (1998) describes some girls as being object "hungry", desiring fulfilment (p. 421).

Renaming the Female 'Oedipus' Complex

Proposals have been made for the need to have a different myth or story that represents the unique dynamics for girls, rather than stick to Oedipus. As Kulish and Holtzman (2008) point out, Freud attempted to fit ideas about female sexuality to the tale of Oedipus, a male, by formulating the girl as initially 'masculine' in her gender. They thus state that to refer to the 'female Oedipus complex' is "a blatant oxymoron" (p. 1). They point out that while Freud recognised the little girl's fear of loss of love from the mother, he regarded this only as an aspect of the girl's pre-Oedipal bond with her mother, rather than a key dynamic of the girl's triadic situation with mother and father. It is this aspect that Kulish and Holtzman formulate as a motivating force of the girl's complex.

Kulish and Holtzman argue that another name is needed to describe the girl's conflicts arising out of her triadic situation. Others have suggested myths that have been argued to be more suited to the story of the girl, such as the myth of Electra or Antigone, and even the fairy tale of Cinderella. I will not outline these here; Kulish and Holtzman provide brief summaries of these formulations and other suggestions that have been made. They argue that these suggested myths and fairy tales may capture some features of the triadic dynamic (e.g. incestuous wishes), but do not capture the broader dynamics that are specific to the girl's situation. They propose 'the *Persephone* Complex' as a name to be used to refer to the complexes of girls related to the dynamics of their triadic situation.

The Greek myth of Persephone is the story of the daughter of Zeus, king of the gods, and his wife Demeter (also his sister), goddess of grain. They name their daughter Kore (which means 'maiden'). One day while gathering flowers in the meadow with some other girls, Kore gets abducted by her uncle Hades, god of the dead, who takes her into his kingdom, the underworld. No one sees her abduction or hears her cries. Demeter, bereft and grief-stricken, descends from Olympus and searches the earth trying to find her daughter, Kore. Her grief causes droughts and famines on earth. Kore later appears in the myth as Hades' wife,

Persephone, queen of the underworld. Kore, the virgin (maiden) has now become Persephone, wife and queen. Zeus tries to persuade Hades to release Kore/Persephone. An agreement is reached that Persephone can be released only if she does not eat in the underworld. Hades, however, tricks Persephone into eating a pomegranate seed, and so Persephone is bound to Hades. A compromise is then reached that Persephone can spend two-thirds of the year with Demeter and one-third of the year with Hades as queen of the underworld.

Some important features of the myth that are worth pointing out are the themes of incest, depictions of sex (symbolised by the taking of the 'seed'), theme of marriage represented by the name change from Kore to Persephone (as in the traditional practice of the wife taking her husband's surname in marriage), and, most importantly, the relationship between mother and daughter. For Kulish and Holtzman, the myth of Persephone captures the girl's developmental crisis much more than the myth of Oedipus does. They point out how the myth depicts the key themes of separation and reunion of mother and daughter, the girl's loss of virginity and her entry into adult sexuality, her fertility, and the depiction of a compromise formation that resolves the conflicts involving desire, love, and loyalty (2008, pp. 46–47). They summarise that "the tale of Persephone warns that leaving mother's protection exposes the girl to the dangers of sexuality; conversely, to become an adult woman, a girl must leave her mother's domain and enter her own" (p. 47). For them, this story represents the various psychic realities for the girl in her journey into adulthood and adult sexuality.

Kulish and Holtzman, similar to Chodorow (discussed in Chapter 6), argue that the girl's entry into the triangular situation of what Freud refers to as the Oedipus complex does not involve the switch of object from mother to father, but rather the *addition* of an object: "girls retain their desire towards their mothers, while they add other objects – male or female" (p. 68). They go on to argue that in entering the world of genital heterosexuality girls need to balance their desire for the father whilst retaining their attachment and need of their mother. This is a challenging task, as the mother comes to represent both the nurturer as well as the rival, and so the fear of losing her is intensified: it "gives a greater weight to object loss and separation issues" for girls than for boys in the triadic situation (p. 76). In the mix is the girl's fear of retribution from a rival mother, envious of her sexual youth. This theme of the mother's envy is frequently depicted in tales, such as Cinderella or Snow White, with the older, envious woman/mother often depicted as a wicked, evil character. These dynamics are represented in the myth of Persephone for whom a solution needs to be found for her to retain her mother as an attachment figure while adding a new male sexual object. In the myth, a compromise is reached. Kulish and Holtzman argue that a girl's object choice (whether it be heterosexual, homosexual, or bisexual), represents a form of compromise or composite of both mother and father.

I end off this chapter by presenting a composite case study that hopefully brings to light some of the Oedipal dynamics that may be brought to the consulting room by female patients.

Case Study: 'Katherine'

Katherine was a 32-year-old woman who came to psychotherapy because she was, as she described it, "overwhelmed" with feelings of uncertainty and sometimes an anxious dread about something "bad" happening. She had been in a relationship with Peter for the past eight years and they had become engaged three months previously and were to be married in six months. She said she loved Peter, but found herself feeling uncertain about marriage, and felt guilty that she had these feelings. They had met through mutual friends and had instantly liked each other, having a lot in common. Katherine was an interior designer, which she seemed to have great passion for and had dreams of having a successful business, but felt she lacked the confidence to really make a go of it and grow it into a bigger business.

Katherine described having a close family. She had had a fairly privileged upbringing, with her father's family having a successful business. She said that she was closer to her father than her mother. He was a lively, enthusiastic, and engaged figure. She said she had a good relationship with her mother but described her as anxious and preoccupied. Her mother had always seemed busy with social and community events. She had a brother three years older than her, and they had a close relationship, describing him as "a typical older brother" who she felt protected by. She described having had a "happy" childhood but had always felt that her parents had been unhappy. Although they never argued, she did not observe a lot of affection between them. They had had children fairly late in their marriage, and she always wondered whether having children was an attempt on their part to bring them closer together.

She described her relationship with Peter as "good". They had no arguments, had similar interests, and enjoyed each other's company. Their sex life was "OK" she said. Sex had dwindled somewhat, and she attributed this to Peter being stressed about a new, quite demanding job, as well as due to her own anxiety. She added that she felt ambivalent about this. On the one hand it did not trouble her that much, that sex had always been something that was not hugely important to her, but on the other hand she worried about becoming "like her parents"; worried about a future loveless marriage.

After the initial meeting I was struck by how muted everything seemed to be. Although she came across as fairly anxious, and she could articulate areas of uncertainty, I had no sense of the "overwhelming" feelings she had referred to. This was the emotional atmosphere of the sessions for the first year or so of psychotherapy. I noticed how everything seemed to stay in more or less 'neutral'. Any transference interpretations were met with some anxiety, and a need to steer clear from any sort of feelings of conflict or excitement. She brought many stories to sessions. I noticed how when she might say something critical about someone or express frustration or anger towards them, she quickly qualified that by telling me something positive about them. Similarly, whenever she seemed to become excited about something, she tended to quickly qualify it with a "but" statement that tended to neutralise things. I learnt about her interior design work. She seemed to have a talent, describing interesting and vibrant interiors she had done for some clients, but at the same time pointing out perceived flaws in her work. It was notable that it involved colourful and 'alive' interior spaces, which stood in stark contrast to the otherwise muted emotional atmosphere. I found myself feeling impressed by the work she described, and 'excited' for her potential, as did she, but she always seemed to struggle to take the plunge with developing the business.

Over the course of psychotherapy, she and Peter had gotten married, and their relationship had remained steady, and their sex life the same. They had no plans for children. This might reflect her internalisation of a 'loveless' parental couple. Over time I learnt more of her relationship with her parents. She described how her father took "great delight" in her. She had been his "princess" as a girl. As she got older, she found herself being uncomfortable about this, as she felt guilty that she was receiving attention from him, that she felt he was not directing at her mother. She was very aware of a distance between her father and her mother, and suspected that her mother may have been a bit depressed and lonely, occupying herself with community events. Although she had a 'good-enough' relationship with her mother, she experienced her as quite preoccupied, and more engaged outside of the home. She also disclosed that her father could get angry at times, becoming easily frustrated with people. She recalled a period when the family business had gone into some financial trouble and there had been tensions among family members. Her father and his brother had had a terrible argument and fallout over it, which had never been fully repaired.

We came to understand her fear of any 'hot feelings' in relationships, which seemed dangerous to her. In the transference, she feared 'hot feelings' coming into our relationship, whether it be potential conflict or excitement. She had needed to dampen and neutralise her desires to keep relationships 'safe'. Her anxiety about passion and sex was also fuelled by a bad sexual experience she had had at university, where she had met a man at a house party and they had started to passionately kiss, and had gone up to one of the bedrooms in the house where they started to have sex. She described it as exciting, frantic sex, but had suddenly felt overpowered by him and he had been rough in penetrating her. She said it was consensual, but that the penetration had been painful, and she had felt scared. We talked about how this added to her feelings of vulnerability about her sexuality and any 'hot feelings'. As we came to understand these aspects of her childhood and sexual relationships more, she seemed to allow herself to become a bit more 'alive' to feelings, and she also started to plan on expanding her business by employing an assistant.

We see here in this brief case study the sort of conflicts described by Horney, Elise, and Kulish and Holtzman. We might consider here Katherine's conscious as well as unconscious fears of vaginal penetration and damage. Her father's anger also added to her sense of vulnerability. Her desire for her father was met with what she perceived as excitement on his part, stirring feelings of guilt and fear of retaliation from her mother, experienced by her perceived withdrawal (her preoccupation). She sensed her desire to be forbidden, fearing the loss of her mother. A distant and somewhat anxious relationship with her mother also led to her struggles to draw on an internal representation of mother's sexuality, to assist her in confidently inhabiting her own sexual, female body, and her sexuality in relation to men, finding herself in a relationship which was in some ways more akin to a sibling relationship (good companions). In the transference, she was also fearful of any 'hot feelings' and any sort of emotional penetration, attempting to keep us in a neutral, sibling-like relationship. However, it was not as if she lacked any passion. This was sublimated in her work, which was full of colour, vibrant and alive.

Chapter 5

Perspectives from French Psychoanalysis

One key area of focus and exploration in French psychoanalysis is the important influence that unconscious discourses originating from the adult have on the development of the child's sexuality (Perelberg, 2018). Two key figures in French psychoanalysis stand out with this shift of thinking: Jacques Lacan and Jean Laplanche, and this chapter will focus predominantly on their theoretical contributions. Of course, these are not the only two figures in French psychoanalysis, but they are the two that have developed a substantively different perspective, and that are frequently cited. I will also refer to some of the work of André Green and Joyce McDougall. Other French psychoanalysts have also been discussed in other chapters (e.g. Chasseguet-Smirgel).

Lacan and the Oedipus Complex as Cultural Structure

The work of Lacan (2001; and as outlined in Bailly, 2009; and Yadlin-Gadot & Hadar, 2023) presents an important revision of the psychoanalytic theories of Freud, and particularly his conception of the human subject. Before considering his views on the Oedipus complex, we need to briefly understand some key aspects of his broader theory.

The Three Orders of Human Reality

Lacan was interested in language and its functions. Following Freud, he regarded a symptom as a form of language in that

DOI: 10.4324/9781003394471-5

something that is unsaid is felt as pain and so communicated in a physical way. Two key concepts developed by Lacan are the *signifier* and the *signified*. A signifier is an acoustic image, while the signified is a concept. For example, we use words (signifiers) to refer to a concept (the signified). We use words to convey meaning. However, for Lacan, this communication is distorted, as there is often a difference between the words we say and what we mean. Words (or signifiers) also lead us onto other words and signifiers, as happens in free association. For Lacan, the unconscious is structured like a language, containing a series of signifying elements.

Lacan's theory of the human psyche is structured around three orders of human reality: the Imaginary, the Symbolic, and the Real. These three orders co-exist and encompass both external and internal realties. Throughout an individual's life, the three orders interact in a dynamic and volatile way. A baby is born vulnerable and entirely dependent on others for survival. Over time, the baby comes to have a mastery over its body through mimicry in what Lacan called 'the mirror phase'. The baby identifies with an image outside of himself. This can include the image of themselves in an actual mirror or the 'image' of another baby. In identifying with this image, the baby learns to do things with its body that it previously could not do. This process of mastery over its behaviour gives the child entry into the social worlds. However, Lacan argued that because the child is identifying with an image that exists outside of themselves, which differs from their bodily experience, there is a degree of alienation and, subsequently, an aspect of alienation from the self or ego. Lacan calls this identification with an outside image the order of the Imaginary. As well as the image of the self, the child creates images of significant others, with whom the child identifies. Later, Donald Winnicott (1967) was greatly influenced by Lacan's concept of the mirror stage in his articulation of the mother acting as an emotional mirror to the infant.

According to Lacan, the baby is born into a pre-existing social, cultural, and linguistic network involving signifiers. A typical example is how a baby is often given a gendered name before they are even born. These days we also have 'gender reveal parties' with parents announcing the gender of the not-yet-born baby, with an explosion of colour blue or pink. Lacan referred to these net-works as the order of the Symbolic. The Symbolic order is a representational world of cultural symbols, laws, and language. As a child begins to grasp the nuances of language, they're not just learning words but are being introduced to a world of norms, rules, and societal expectations. The order of the Symbolic inter-acts with the mirror phase and the order of the Imaginary. While the child is captured by an image, they will also be aware of the uttered words of others, such as the parents. Thus, the baby will assume signifiers from the words that are uttered from its parents as being elements of the image that it identifies with. Thus, the child's identification with an image is not just imaginary, but also symbolic, and may contain, in the unconscious, an identification with a symbolic ideal. For example, we often comment on how a baby looks 'just like' their mother or their father. Developmentally then, the child moves from the order of the Imaginary to the order of the Symbolic.

The order of the Real is difficult to define. Lacan referred to the Real as being that which cannot be symbolised. What we would speak of as our 'reality' is usually a mixture of the Imaginary and the Symbolic, the two orders that involve representation. A sig-nifier may represent something, but not in its entirety. What is 'left over' is the Real. For Lacan, the Real is that which is excluded from our reality; that which is without representation and mean-ing and that we fail to be aware of and explore. The Real includes basic physical, bodily experience that cannot be symbolised.

Lacan made a distinction between the 'ego' and the 'subject', relating the ego to the Imaginary, and the subject to the Symbolic. He draws on the work of Klein on symbolism and the develop-ment of the ego (Klein, 1930) to explain how language constitutes the subject. As the symbolic world of signifiers pre-exists the birth of the child, it can be regarded as a social and cultural structure into which the child is born and learns to take its place. For Lacan, an individual's identity involves forms of otherness, and the aim of analysis is for the ego to be integrated with the Sym-bolic, the historical social cultural structures that they are born into. In this, Lacan was inspired by the work of the French anthropologist Claude Lévi-Strauss (discussed briefly in Chapter

8). For Lacan, the Oedipus complex is experienced within an anthropological structure that a child is born into. He suggested that the Oedipus complex is situated primarily in the order of the Symbolic, where the child enters the world of language and of law. The Oedipus complex thus is already present, in the psyche of the child's parents, even before the child is born. The parents, for example, have fantasies, wishes, and expectations about their forthcoming baby.

Lacan's Formulation of the Oedipus Complex

Lacan viewed marriage and the family as an organisation that forms part of a larger symbolic organisation. The man/father and woman/mother become part of this symbolic structure, organising men's relation to women and depicting rules of hierarchy differentiating children and parents. Lacan distinguished between the real, biological father, from the symbolic aspects of the father, which he referred to as the Name-of-the-Father ("*le nom du père*"). The Name-of-the-Father is not the real name of the father but rather serves a symbolic function of paternity. The Name-of the-Father represents society's laws and restrictions as communicated through language. Mitchell (1974) stated how this symbolic father is also the dead ancestral father murdered by the primal horde, described by Freud in *Totem and Taboo* (see Chapter 8).

According to Lacan, in the Oedipus complex, the child must separate from the relationship with the mother and enter the world of the symbolic that involves three terms: the mother, the child, and the object of mother's desire, which Lacan referred to as the 'phallus'. The 'phallus' here does not equate to the penis, rather it represents the penis and the symbolic idea of loss or lack. He proposed that the Oedipus complex involves three moments. At first is the child and mother in a maternal matrix in which there is an imaginary wholeness, with all needs and desires seemingly satisfied. Lacan links to Freud's formulation of female sexuality as the child equating for the mother with the desired-for penis from her own pre-Oedipal period. In the second moment, the child comes to learn that he or she is not identical to the object that the mother desires, as much as they at first imagine themselves to be and try to be. The child becomes aware of the mother having another object of desire (the father), a desire that is signified by her absences. This other object (the father) seems to possess something which the mother desires, that the child comes to realise they do not have. In the third moment, the father is perceived as being the one having what the mother desires, which becomes symbolised as the phallus. The father, as the perceived bearer of the phallus, intervenes in that the child cannot take his place and be the phallus for the mother. The mother also intervenes by calling up the Name-of-the-Father. The child comes to know that they cannot be the desired phallus for the mother and faces symbolic castration: the child gives up the phallus as an imaginary object, and it becomes instead a signifier for that which is missing. For the boy, he will accept this fact in the knowledge that there is a phallus that he will one day possess. For the girl, she will accept the loss of the phallus and hope to receive it in the future from a man and in having a baby of her own.

In this third term, the child also comes to know that the father has the phallus, but ultimately, authority lies with the symbolic father, an authority that the child's father also is subject to. As Hartke (2016) states:

> the child perceives that the mother has no phallus, that the child is neither the phallus nor does she have one. The father does have the phallus, but he is not the phallus. The phallus is an institution situated in the culture, and based on this institution everyone is symbolically castrated.

> (p. 904)

The phallus is thus a signifier of loss, an unfulfillable desire, and represents a core lack in both femininity and masculinity.

The resolution of the Oedipus complex also involves the child's submission to the symbolic authority of the Name-of-the-Father, and the acceptance of limitations. By recognising the boundaries set by the Symbolic order through the resolution of the Oedipus complex, the child learns to negotiate their desires, understanding that some can be fulfilled while others must be repressed or transformed.

Rosine Perelberg (2015), partly influenced by the work of Lacan, makes an important distinction between the 'murdered father' and the 'dead father'. She defines the concept of the 'murdered father' as representing an omnipotent, narcissistic fantasy where, by killing the father, the individual assumes the father's place as the phallus, and takes possession of the women. In contrast, the 'dead father' refers to the father of the symbolic order and the institution of law. The 'dead father' is more powerful than the real father and constitutes what Perelberg refers to as the internal paternal function, a symbolic third (p. 12). She describes the progression from the murdered father fantasy to the establishment of the 'dead father' in the resolution of the Oedipus complex as a critical developmental task, regulating desire and aggression, and establishing the incest taboo. This enables the child to enter the social and cultural sphere.

The Oedipus Complex as Triangular Structure

André Green (2004), like Lacan, regards the Oedipus complex as a pre-existing structure into which the child is born. For Green, the Oedipus complex is created by the child's parents, who themselves have experienced it in their own lives. He suggests that the mother–infant relationship is never just a dyad, as the presence of a third exists in the mind of the mother, that is her partner. The mother's partner is also a physical presence; in the support the partner gives to the mother in childcare. This presence is not a direct presence for the child, as the infant is still incapable of perceiving separate, whole objects, but is nevertheless conveyed to the child via the unconscious of the mother. Green states:

> I do not think that one has to wait until the child is capable of conceiving of the third person (through language, for instance) before acknowledging that the child can be influenced by fantasies in the mother's mind about the father. I propose to call this phenomenon the *other of the object* (that which is not the subject). The element of the third is not restricted to the person of the father; it is also symbolic.
>
> (p. 104; italics in original)

Green (2004) follows on the work of Lacan and his conception of the father existing as a signifier in the mind of the mother. As noted earlier, Perelberg (2015) refers to this as the paternal function that exists in the mind of the mother. Furthermore, when the mother is in an intimate presence with the baby (e.g. breastfeeding), the tenderness of the moment may also be mixed up with sensuality, given the mother's sexual relationship with the father, that is present in her mind. This is an aspect emphasised by Laplanche (discussed below). According to Green, in such a moment, a part of the mother is absent to the child. For Green, there is thus an Oedipal triangular structure from the start, but this is an 'open' triangle at first; open because it is only the mother who has a relationship with both the father and the child (Hartke, 2016). As the father is gradually discovered as a separate, whole object, this 'open' triangular situation develops into a closed triangle structure. As the child starts to understand the relational link between mother and father, this then becomes an Oedipal triangular situation (similar to what Britton described – see Chapter 3).

Laplanche and the Enigmatic of Sexuality

Again, before we consider Laplanche's perspectives on the Oedipus complex, we need to briefly understand some of his broader theory of sexuality.

The Sexual Instinct and the Sexual Drive

Laplanche, like Lacan, sought 'a return to Freud' by retranslating and reinterpreting some of Freud's theoretical ideas. One of Laplanche's (1976, 2011) areas of translation involved his carefully distinguishing between instinct and drive. Freud referred to these two distinct terms in his writing – *Instinkt* and *Trieb*. However, Strachey, in his translation of Freud's work, translated the word *Trieb* as 'instinct', rather than 'drive'. As a result, the concept of 'instinct' was most used in the psychoanalytic vocabulary. This has since been revised by Mark Solms in his contemporary translations of Freud's work – *The Revised Standard Edition*.

Laplanche (1976, 2011) stressed as important the differences between the sexual 'instinct' and the sexual 'drive'. He distinguishes between: (1) the self-preservation instinct, which is not sexual, (2) infantile sexuality, which involves the sexual drive, and (3) the sexual instinct, which is expressed in puberty. Laplanche defines the concept of instinct, as Freud seemed to have considered it, as referring to the animal instincts, and is hereditary and adaptive. The sexual instinct corresponds to puberty and genital maturation and an innate tendency towards having sex. According to him, the sexual instinct is pre-programmed towards the self-preservation of the human species. Laplanche linked the sexual drive to infantile sexuality, which he regarded as Freud's greatest discovery. The sexual drive is not innate. It is a sexuality that involves pleasure and desire, and, as Freud stated, is 'polymorphously perverse'. However, the sexual drive 'leans on' the self-preservation instinct, which involves attachment and affection, and so it is also object-orientated, not just auto-erotic.

The sexual instinct is absent, it is in latency, between birth and puberty. The sexual drive, meanwhile, is situated in the period between birth and puberty (infantile sexuality), although the sexual drive is repressed and goes into a period of latency between the stage of the Oedipus complex and puberty. Thus, during the period of latency of the sexual instinct, the sexual drive "has free reign" (Laplanche, 2011, p. 19). According to Laplanche, the source of the sexual drive is in the unconscious (as observed by Freud). However, he critiques the notion of an endogenous infantile sexuality, that is a sexuality that originates from within the infant. According to him, infantile sexuality originates from without, from the enigmatic seductions of the sexual adult. These seductions he describes as a kind of interference or 'noise' and has also been described as an 'excess' (Scarfone, 2013). I'll discuss this in more detail below. It is these seductions which make the sexual drive emerge from the instinct to be expressed in infantile sexuality. If we consider again the myth of Oedipus, it is his father (Laius) who sets off the chain of events for Oedipus, as a result of his sexual seduction of Chrysippus, leading to a curse and the parents' decision to banish their child, and it is his mother, Jocasta, that can be said to have seduced Oedipus (Zepf et al.,

2016). Thus, the sexual complex that Oedipus later finds himself in is triggered by the adult sexuality and actions of his parents. Zepf and colleagues (2016) argue that the sort of primal seduction that Laplanche speaks of includes the "unconscious sexual signals springing from unresolved parental Oedipal conflicts" (p. 703).

Laplanche does not see the sexual instinct, as it manifests in puberty, as a continuation of infantile sexuality and the drive, but rather as "a qualitatively new development" (2011, p. 22). He dismisses Freud's formulation of the psychosexual stages, arguing that the sexual instinct and the sexual drive differ, the one does not develop out of the other. He argues that the sexuality of the drive, a sexuality that is acquired during the infantile period, comes *before* the sexual instinct in puberty, the sexuality that is innate. As he describes: "*Drive comes before instinct*, fantasy comes before function; and when the sexual instinct arrives, the seat is already occupied" (2011, p. 22; italics in original). In puberty and adulthood, pre-genital pleasures have to be integrated with genital pleasures and adult sexuality.

Sexuality and the 'Adult–Infans' Relationship

Freud abandoned his theory of seduction for understanding hysteria and neurosis, with the discovery of infantile sexuality and the Oedipus complex. Laplanche (2011) reintroduces seduction, the intervention of the adult, but of a form much different to that which Freud had initially considered. He states that such seductions from the adult is not something contingent or pathological (as in the case of sexual abuse) but rather is an inevitable part of what he terms the adult–*infans* relationship, which he describes as the "fundamental anthropological situation" (p. 99). He describes the infantile sexual drive as "an endless search" that cannot be gratified, and "knows nothing of satisfaction by means of the adapted complimentary object; it always lacks sufficient binding and is ambivalent" (p. 21). The Oedipus complex occurs as "the major attempt at binding" in infantile sexuality (p. 21). I'll come back to discussing the 'fundamental anthropological situation' and the Oedipus complex below.

As mentioned earlier, Laplanche states that the sexual drive 'leans on' the self-preservation instinct for support. He recognises *attachment* as an important component of the self-preservation instinct, in that the infant needs the adult to survive. The attachment figure (mother, father, or other adult) provides warmth and nourishment, and the attachment relationship is supported by communication between the infant and adult. Laplanche stresses that this communication in the attachment relationship is at first not linguistic but involves unconscious communication. The adult–*infans* situation reactivates the infantile sexual unconscious of the adult, and so some of the messages that are communicated from the adult to the child belong to the sexual unconscious of the adult. Such communications stem from the adult's sexual unconscious, they are compromised, and cannot be made sense of, by both adult and child, and so they are 'enigmatic'. This enigmatic communication requires translation, or symbolisation, by the child, and it is in this process of translation that the sexual drive and infantile sexuality emerges. For example, in the infant's relation to the mother's breast, Laplanche states that there are two processes at play. There is the self-preservation instinct and attachment which facilitates the infant's need for nutrition: the infant has a need for food, and the mother's breast is the object that provides this. For Freud, there is no communication here other than the material provision of food. The experience of sexuality derives from the satisfaction experienced by the child. However, Laplanche critiques this idea, arguing that for this to be so, something sexual is required to exist from the start. Instead, he suggests that the infant's first experience with the breast is self-preservatory. However, the experience is made more complex by what is communicated by the mother, a sexual adult:

> What matters is the introduction of the sexual element, not from the side of physiology of the infant but from the side of messages from the adult. To put it concretely, these messages are located on the side of the breast, the *sexual breast of the woman*, the inseparable companion of the milk of 'self-preservation'.
>
> (Laplanche, 2011, p. 69)

Scarfone (2013) invites us to imagine the infant asking: "What does this breast want from me as it gets excited in suckling me and excites me though I cannot understand why?" (p. 94). The mother also transmits messages from her adult, sexual unconscious mind, when she physically caresses, touches, and holds her baby. Some of these enigmatic messages the infant attempts to translate, which is the source for the emergence of the sexual drive. That which cannot be translatable is repressed and remains as elements of the unconscious. From this perspective, sexuality can always be considered to involve an enigmatic 'otherness', and the relationship to the sexual object involves the desire for the otherness of the object, regardless of the biological sex of the subject and object (Stein, 1998a).

An interesting and important point that Laplanche makes is regarding the primacy of gender over sex difference. Freud regarded the observed anatomical differences between the sexes as foundational on the development of gender and sexual identity. Laplanche challenges this, by arguing that biological sex is not, and cannot be accurately perceived and understood by the very young child. Instead, it is gender that is first perceived; not an organised conception of gender, but rather as an enigmatic message deriving from the adult. As he observes, the baby is assigned a gender at birth, they are assigned a name and a position in the kinship network. The process of assigning gender is not a discrete act but rather is ongoing and constituted through various communications from adult to child, involving signifiers of gender. These messages are communicated consciously and unconsciously through verbal as well as behavioural means (through the administration of bodily care, for example). It is these messages that the child first encounters, before they become aware of the anatomical differences between the sexes. Laplanche suggests then that the child does not identify as a gender but rather is *identified* as a gender by the adult (Scarfone, 2013), and the child's later observation of the anatomical differences between the sexes provides a code in which to translate the meaning of this gender allocation.

The 'Fundamental Anthropological Situation' and the Oedipus Complex

As mentioned earlier, the 'fundamental anthropological situation' involves what Laplanche refers to as "the adult–*infans* relation" (2011, p. 102), which is made up of an adult with his or her sexual unconscious which includes elements of their infantile, perverse sexuality, and the infant who is "not equipped with any genetic sexual organisation or any hormonal activators of sexuality" (p. 102) and initially has no sexual fantasies (p. 204). For Laplanche, the fundamental anthropological situation can exist between an infant and other adults that form part of their environment, not just the parents.

Laplanche (2011) states that the Oedipus complex, which is a *familial* situation, does not equate to his notion of the fundamental anthropological situation. He argues that the Oedipus complex may be generally found, but it is not universal, it is a mythical narrative that the child may unconsciously use to help make sense of their triangular relationship to his parents, but it is not necessarily present in the fundamental anthropological situation. What is most important about this situation is communication and the enigmatic messages received by the infant from the adult. Such messages can only be interpreted later in retrospect; each is "a message awaiting translation" (p. 107). The child attempts to translate such messages by drawing on 'codes', or "performed narrative schemas" (p. 217) which exist within his familial, social, and cultural environment. The Oedipus complex is such a narrative. Laplanche furthermore dismissed the notion of a hereditary Oedipus complex centred on the murder of the primal father by his sons (as proposed by Freud in *Totem and Taboo*). While he accepts that an Oedipal structure that prohibits incest may exist culturally, he does not agree that it exists phylogenetically in the unconscious of the infant. He does not position the Oedipus complex as that which is repressed, as does Freud, but rather as a narrative that does the repressing of the sexual and instigates the order of law.

According to Laplanche, in adolescence, the sexual instinct seeks its complementarity in the erogenous zones, while the sexual drive of infancy is different. As Freud outlined in *The Ego and the Id*, there is a complete Oedipus complex in infantile sexuality, involving same-sex and opposite-sex desire, and hostility towards the rival parent. Laplanche states that in adolescence, there are thus two sexual currents at play, the sexual drive and the sexual instinct, and in this period, there are "two Oedipuses, one of which is 'complimentary' while the other is irremediably bisexual and, at the same time, ambivalent" (2011, p. 23).

Ruth Stein (1998b) proposes we might look at Freud's and Laplanche's theories about sexuality as a "tension arc" (p. 262), with on the one end the pleasures of bodily excitation and stimulation, and on the other end, the unattainable enigmatic object that is desired and sought. She suggests that sexuality is something both embodied and displaced.

Some Further Developments on Psychic Bisexuality

Joyce McDougall (1995), a New Zealand–French psychoanalyst, like Horney and Klein before her, disagrees with Freud's assertion that it is only in the phase of the Oedipus complex (the phallic stage) that the child comes to observe the anatomical differences between the sexes. The child has an awareness of the vagina as well as the penis from an early age, and the experience of difference, including sex difference, is anxiety-provoking from the start. McDougall accepts Stoller's (1968) concept of a 'core gender identity', arguing that a child needs to renunciate their bisexual longings and accept their monosexuality, and develop a 'masculine' or 'feminine' self-identity. She argues that the traits of 'masculine' and 'feminine' are not biologically determined; they are shaped by the parental unconscious and social-cultural norms.

McDougall develops Freud's conception of psychic bisexuality to make the observation that, rather than the child having desire for one parent at a time, the child has both parents, wanting the love of each parent, and "to possess the mysterious sexual organs and fantasized power of both father and mother, man and woman" (1995, p. xi). The girl envies the penis of the boy, and the boy envies the vagina of the girl. She further points out that the boy too suffers penis envy; that is the larger penis of his father that he does not possess. Both the girl and the boy are envious of the mother's "magical power to attract Father's penis and make the babies whom the two parents desire" (p. 5). McDougall observes the co-existence of homosexual and heterosexual desire, and describes the existence of two homosexual 'currents' that exist in the unconscious of everyone: firstly, the desire for the same-sex parent, and secondly, the wish to be the opposite-sex parent. The child has to relinquish some of their bisexual longings, with the result that these early desires will remain unfulfilled. As McDougall describes:

> the little girl will not become a man, will never possess her mother sexually, will never make babies with her, and will never receive a baby from her father. Likewise the little boy will not become a woman and will never make babies with his father or become his father's sexual partner, as he had once imagined.
>
> (1995, p. xiv)

McDougall argues that children must come to accept their monosexuality; that is that they cannot be both sexes and cannot possess both parents. This is experienced as a narcissistic wound and involves having to mourn that which cannot be had. Thus, for McDougall, sexuality has a traumatic dimension. As a result of these unfulfilled bisexual desires, the child in the end has an ambivalent attachment to both parents, involving love as well as envy and hatred. The girl has to identify with her mother but also continues to be dependent on her, needing her support and guidance for some time.

O'Connor and Ryan (1993) critique McDougall's largely heteronormative stance which suggests that only heterosexual desire is 'real desire', and homosexual desire illusory and needing to be relinquished. She had initially suggested that the failure to accept the 'truth' of heterosexual reality is a perversion. McDougall reneged on some of her earlier generalisations made about female homosexuality (1995, p. 38) and argued that both heterosexuality and homosexuality needed explanation.

Chapter 6

Relational Perspectives on the Oedipus Complex

Since Freud, there has been a general shift in focus to the early maternal relationship, or 'pre-Oedipal' relationship, and the quality of that relationship as important for understanding psychological development. The shift in focus from the Oedipal phase to this 'pre-Oedipal' maternal relationship has been described as a move away from a consideration of sexuality as a central dimension of personality development (Green, 1995) to an emphasis on attachment. However, Klein brought Oedipal dynamics right into the first year of life, and as Dimen (1999) argues, many contemporary, relational psychoanalytic perspectives develop from this suggestion from Klein, and so, she argues, "as individuals, we are no longer thought to go straight from birth to Oedipus. On the way, we pass through, even tarry a while in and definitely *take our sexual shapes from*, a maternal landscape" (p. 418; italics added). She states that "sexuality has become a relation, not a force" (p. 418).

In this chapter I will discuss some important contributions from what I broadly categorise as 'relational' approaches (that is, approaches that focus on the interpersonal, emotional aspects of the parent–child relationship and the development of the self). There are many theories that could have been included, and I have chosen to focus on authors that have had more to say about the Oedipus complex. I will start by discussing theories that have focused on the mother–child relationship and implications for the Oedipus complex. I will then look at some theories that consider in more detail the triangular relationships of the Oedipus complex. Other relational theorists have also been discussed in other chapters.

DOI: 10.4324/9781003394471-6

A Deeper Focus on the Mother–Child Relationship

There is a vast amount of psychoanalytic literature that focuses on the mother–child relationship and its importance for psychological development. I will discuss here the important contributions of two American psychoanalysts: Nancy Chodorow, who takes a more object-relations approach, and Jessica Benjamin, who introduces an intersubjective approach. Both focus on the dynamics of individuation and separation. I will focus on what they say about this in relation to the Oedipus complex.

Chodorow on Mothering, Gender, and Mother–Child Separation

Chodorow (1978), in her book *The Reproduction of Mothering*, made an important contribution to a feminist psychoanalytic examination of female subjectivity, and, particularly, mothering. That is, the act of nurturing and caring for children which is historically primarily performed by women. As many others do, Chodorow observes the prevalence of a gendered division of labour, and she puts forward an argument that, while women have the biological capacity for childbearing, the performance of mothering is socially and culturally reproduced, rather than biologically determined. She argues that the quality of the mother–child relationship prepares women for mothering and men for their primary participation in work. For example, she states:

> Women, as mothers, produce daughters with mothering capacities and the desire to mother. These capacities and needs are built into and grow out of the mother–daughter relationship itself. By contrast, women as mothers (and men as not-mothers) produce sons whose nurturant capacities and needs have been systematically curtailed and repressed.
>
> (Chodorow, 1978, p. 7)

While societal expectations for mothers and fathers may have changed since the era of Freud in societies of Europe and North America, and fathers are more involved in the care of children than before, this gendered division of labour remains prominent.

This was certainly the case at the time that Chodorow was writing. She argued that women mother children within this social and cultural structure of the gendered division of labour, and in turn, this "produces in daughters and sons a division of psychological capacities which leads them to reproduce this sexual and familial division of labor" (1978, p. 7). Chodorow dismisses the notion of a 'mothering instinct', and she also critiques feminist arguments that claim that women are behaviourally and cognitively 'trained' into the role of mothering. She argues that such arguments tend to define mothering or parenting as constituting a set of behaviours. For Chodorow, mothering or parenting is fundamentally inter-personal and interactive and involves participation in an "affective relationship" (p. 33). This requires relational capacities that cannot be taught or learnt; rather, they are internalised and "built into personality" (p. 39). Thus, for Chodorow, the reproduction of mothering requires a psychoanalytic explanation.

In infancy, the baby is at first totally dependent on the care of the parent. Because it is typically women who are allocated the role of primary caretaker, the infant is thus mostly dependent on the mother. Thus, Chodorow emphasises that it is the quality of *her* care and *her* presence and absence that is internalised as the infant's earliest experience (p. 61). She draws on object relations theories to describe the developmental process that the infant takes from a state of complete dependence and merger with the primary caregiver, through a growing awareness and tolerance for separation of self from object, to gradually more independence. Where the primary caregiver is the mother, the father and older siblings typically come in here as external figures, and the mother's relationship with them represents an external reality that the child must come to terms with. During this process, anxieties about loss and survival, conflicting feelings of love and hate towards the loving and frustrating mother, and feelings of jealousy and rivalry are evoked and defended against. Chodorow, like many other more relational theorists, understands such anxieties, conflicts, and ambivalences as arising out of this mother–infant relationship, as well as the later Oedipal relationship.

As relational psychoanalytic theorists point out, it is this early mother–child relationship, which is hopefully 'good-enough' (Winnicott, 1965) in its quality, that enables the child to develop a sense of self. The child, of course, does also have a relationship with the father, but in infancy he is typically more of a separate figure than the mother is. This is quite different to Freud's formulation that places the father, and the phallus, as the more influential figure. Chodorow goes on to argue that the early mother–child mothering relationship "creates specific conscious and unconscious attitudes or expectations in children" about gender (1978, p. 83). She argues that the child's relationship to the mother differs significantly for boys and girls, and that the development of the sense and activity of mothering in girls, and not in boys, "results from differential object-relational experiences, and the ways these are internalized and organized" (p. 91); differences which are found in the pre-Oedipal period and strengthen in the Oedipal period.

Mothering and the Oedipus Complex

Chodorow suggests that the Oedipus complex for girls does not just involve the girl relinquishing her mother as desired object and transferring her desire onto her father, as Freud suggested. Rather, her relationship to her father is *added on* to her continuing relationship to her mother with whom she remains identified (1978, p. 93). For the boy, the mother remains the primary object of desire, although he has to disidentify and separate from her and identify with the father. The girl's pre-Oedipal relationship with her mother is more prolonged than it is for the boy. Chodorow argues that because boys must separate from their mothers in a way that girls do not, they experience themselves as more separate and as having more defined boundaries than girls do. Girls retain an element of 'merger' with their mothers and so have more permeable boundaries between self and other. As a result, she claims, girls have more complex relational capabilities than boys do. Furthermore, the mother, in this early relationship period, experiences and treats the boy differently to how she experiences and treats the girl. She does not regard this as something that is innately driven. The differences in mothering are expressed in the mother's conscious and unconscious affective and attitudinal relation to her child, seeing the girl as more like herself, an extension of herself, and the boy as more 'other' to herself, a male other with whom she may be more seductive: she "may push her son out of his preoedipal relationship to her into an oedipally toned relationship defined by its sexuality and gender distinction" (p. 107).

In addition to these differences in the pre-Oedipal period, the child's family setting "creates a different endopsychic situation" (1978, p. 111) for the girl than for the boy during the Oedipal period. Chodorow points out that for both girls and boys, hetero-sexuality and heterosexual identifications are the assumed, pre-ferred outcome of the Oedipus complex; an assumption and normative preference that is derived from social relationships and imposed on individuals. It is not to be considered self-evident or as the 'natural' sexuality. She understands (hetero)sexual orienta-tion to be "enforced and constructed by parents. Parents are usually heterosexual and sexualize their relationship to children of either gender accordingly, employing socially sanctioned child-rearing practices" (p. 113).

Chodorow suggests that the girl enters the triangular Oedipal situation later than the boy does, due to the prolonged pre-Oedipal relationship to her mother. For the girl, what happens in the Oedipal period builds on this pre-Oedipal relationship. She critiques the formulations provided by Horney, Klein, and Chasseguet-Smirgel (discussed in Chapters 3 and 4) and others, which she feels give us a limited explanation for the girl's turn from her mother to her father as object of desire, which is based on an assumed innate heterosexuality; that the girl desires the penis for her own gratification. Chodorow suggests that one of the reasons why the girl may turn to her father from her mother is that the father may encourage stereotypical heterosexual behaviour in their children, more so than mothers do, and so encourage stereotypically feminine behaviours in their daughters and in their father–daughter relationship. Thus, she considers the "possible part played by a father in wooing a girl, but not a boy" (p. 120). Furthermore, the father is perceived as a figure who can help the girl get away from the more enmeshed relationship she has with her omnipotent pre-Oedipal mother than a boy is per-ceived as having. And so, part of the Oedipal dynamic for the girl is a change in the intensity of relationship with the mother.

Chodorow's account of the resolution of the Oedipus complex for boys and for girls differs from the formulation offered by Freud. For her, it is not castration anxiety that accounts for the resolution of the Oedipus complex through the relinquishment and repression of incestuous desire, but rather the nature of the boy's Oedipal relationship to his mother, and, for the girl, her relationship with her father. For the boy, the intensity of the mother–son bond is experienced as a threat to his sense of masculine independence. Additionally, the intensity of this bond causes some envy for the father, who sees his son as a rival in a way that he does not perceive his daughter to be. For the boy, it is these dynamics that lead to the repression of his desire for his mother. For the girl, her bond with her father is not as intense as the boy's bond to his mother, because it is mitigated by her relationship and dependence on her mother. It also comes at a later stage, following an initial pre-Oedipal bond with her mother. Because her desire for her father is less intense and the threat of retaliation from her mother is less present, her Oedipal desire for her father does not have to be repressed as much. For the girl, there continues to be some elements of an Oedipal conflict and triangulation through puberty and into adulthood, until she gives up her Oedipal investments on her parents and transfers these onto other relationships in adulthood. Most boys, on the other hand, because of the intensity of Oedipal feelings in relation to both parents, have had to repress and resolve the Oedipal complex earlier and are "more ready to turn to the nonfamilial external world in a search for important objects" (1978, p. 134).

As a result of these differing mothering experiences, and the different Oedipal relationships experienced by boys and girls, most boys separate from their mothers, and parents, more than girls, and tend to grow away from their families and into the public sphere and the world of work, more so than women who remain more in a domestic sphere than men do (p. 38). And so, the differently developed affective and relational capabilities for mothering along the lines of gender, and consequent mothering by women, is reproduced.

Chodorow (2012), in reflecting back on her influential book, describes it as "a generalizing book" (p. 54), describing "a pattern" (p. 59) of what she regarded as typical dynamics and relationships, but pointed out that there would be some variance. She further acknowledges that the book assumed generalisations of a Western, white, middle-class heterosexual family structure, which she had subsequently addressed in later writings. However, in the book, she describes what she regarded as "a statistically prevalent" model of family that needed explaining at the time (p. 56). One of Chodorow's (1992) important arguments was that heterosexuality itself needed explaining, regarding it as "a compromise formation" (p. 267).

Benjamin's Intersubjective Model

In her book, *The Bonds of Love*, Benjamin (1988) introduces to psychoanalysis the 'intersubjective view', which she distinguishes from the 'intrapsychic'. She states that an intersubjective view,

> maintains that the individual grows in and through the rela-
> tionship to other subjects. Most importantly, this perspective
> observes that the other whom the self meets is also a self, a
> subject in his or her own right. It assumes that we are able
> and need to recognize that other subject as different and yet
> alike, as an other who is capable of sharing similar mental
> experience. Thus the idea of intersubjectivity reorients the
> conception of the psychic world from a subject's relations to
> its object toward a subject meeting another subject.
>
> (pp. 19–20)

Recognition and Differentiation

Benjamin interpreted Freud's work, as formulated perhaps most clearly in the Oedipus complex, as a conflict between instinct and civilisation. She expanded on this conflict by exploration of the relationship and conflict between love and domination. She challenges the central assumptions about gender, authority, and power that underpin Freud's theory, proposing a more intersubjective model that explains how domination and submission emerge in relationships, rather than are imposed on relationships. In her view, development is not solely based on the acceptance of hierarchical authority and a submission to this, but rather development is based on the ability to recognise and be recognised by others as independent subjects. This perspective shifts the focus from a paternalistic, authority-based model to one that is relational and based on the co-construction of identity.

Benjamin (1988) conceived of 'domination' as "a two-way process, a system involving the participation of those who submit to power as well as those who exercise it", and how 'domination' becomes internalised or "anchored" in the minds of the dominated (p. 5). She draws on feminist criticism of a male-dominated psychoanalysis that emphasises the authority of the father, to reconsider domination in terms of beginning with the infant's relationship with its mother, the 'first bond', and the conflict between dependence and independence that the child experiences in relation to her. This early experience develops into issues of love and domination in adult erotic life, and how this becomes associated with the anatomical differences between the sexes and notions of masculinity and femininity.

Benjamin also focuses on the development of ego and its objects, rather than on Freud's focus on drives and defences. For Benjamin, what is key in this early period is the process of 'differentiation', where the child develops a self, with an awareness of its distinctness from others; a recognition and acknowledgement of difference. In turn, our own need for recognition from others is dependent on the recognition that others are different and separate to the self (1988, p. 12). This process of recognition and differentiation occurs from the beginning with the first communications between the mother and infant, communications delivered through touch, sounds, feelings, and facial expressions. Such communication is intersubjective, in that it includes the conscious and unconscious reciprocal communications between mother and infant. Benjamin states how for the mother a 'paradox' exists, in that while there is the knowledge and recognition that the baby has come from her, she does not yet know who this baby is, the self of the baby. Thus, the mother's emotional and psychological connection with her baby contains some conflict around recognition and misrecognition, and a sense of loss that the baby, although coming from her, is not her, and gradually, as it develops will become more themselves. There are conflicting experiences of togetherness and otherness. So too for the baby. At first in an undifferentiated state with the mother, the infant gradually comes to separate from their mother. Their needs are frequently gratified, but at other times not.

For Benjamin (1988), the mother is the first attachment figure and, later, the first object of desire. But this relationship exists with a range of conflicting feelings. As well as a provider and caregiver, she is also a reinforcer of limits. She is not there just to meet the demands of the child, but is also a real, separate other, with her own subjectivity. In order for the mother to recognise, facilitate, and allow for their child's need for separateness and growing independence, she has to also recognise her own separateness and independent self. She must be the 'not-me' for the child (p. 24). However, this process is fraught with emotional conflicts for the mother, as it is for the child. The child comes to understand themselves as a separate, independent self. However, they need, and are dependent on, the other to recognise that. Where there has been a positive experience of mutual recognition and gradual separation in childhood, there is a greater capacity for mutuality in adulthood; the capacity to enter into the psychological space of the other and allow the other in. This is the basis of a fulfilling erotic adult relationship: "both partners lose themselves in each other without loss of self" (p. 29). Where the early mutual recognition has gone awry, a more defensive boundary between the internal and external forms. Benjamin offers this as an alternate model to Freud's psychosexual stages of development, emphasising conflicts and "tensions *between interacting individuals* rather than that *within the individual*" (p. 29; italics in original).

The process of the child's separation and differentiation from mother (and father) is a process which contains within it a struggle for domination. As the young child, who wants it all, attempts to assert their, often grandiose, wishes and demands, this is met with the limit-setting and demands of the parent. But equally, this process comes with fear, as the child, still dependent on the adult, fears his or her parents' abandonment. The mother (and father) also has to deal with the sense of loss of the all-dependent infant, and her frustrations and need to retaliate against her child's unreasonable demands.

Benjamin (1988) is inspired by Winnicott's (1969) paper, *The Use of the Object*, here. In this paper, Winnicott distinguishes between *relating* to an object and *using* it. Winnicott regards the experience of relating to an object as the first experience to the object, where the object is related to as if an extension of the self, "a bundle of projections" (p. 712). This form of relationship gradually gives way to an appreciation of the object's separateness, a separate object with whom it can enter into an exchange; it can start to use the object. By 'using', Winnicott refers to a healthier, more mature experience with the object that involves a creative relationship and an awareness of a shared reality. For this to occur the object that is at first *related* to must be destroyed, i.e. to place the object outside of him or herself, rather than as existing in fantasy in his or her own mind. The object must 'survive' this destruction in order to be found by the child as an external object that can be used. Thus, for Benjamin, 'destruction' involves the effort to differentiate (p. 38). With the survival of the object, reality (the external, independent object) is discovered, rather than reality being imposed onto the child (as the classical Oedipal model suggests).

Benjamin (1988) sees the tensions and conflicts involved in the process of mutual recognition and differentiation as extending into adult relationship, with a continual "exchange of influence" between experiences of sameness and difference, dependence and independence, harmony and disharmony (p. 49).

Gender Differences in a Child's Differentiation from Mother

Benjamin (1988) observes a fundamental difference when it comes to the boy's and girl's relationship to their mothers, usually their primary object of attachment and of desire. Initially, in the stage of mother–infant merger, all infants at first "feel themselves to be like their mothers" (p. 75). In the process of differentiating and separating from her, boys have to disidentify from their mothers and define themselves as a different sex to them, whereas girls do not have to disidentify with mother in this way. She argues that "male children achieve their masculinity by denying their original identification or oneness with their mothers" (p. 73). This requires their repudiation of their mothers and of femininity. Furthermore, in the process of differentiating himself as different and disidentifying with mother, the male child risks losing his capacity for mutual recognition he had with his mother before. Rather than relating to her intersubjectively, he may instead relate to her, and the female other, as an object. This Benjamin (1988) referred to as "false differentiation" (p. 76), and one that "resounds throughout our culture" (p. 77). Girls, in their process of differentiation, do not need to disidentify with their mothers as boys do, and so for her there may be no obvious "hallmark of separateness" (p. 78). For women, there may develop a denial of subjectivity, of the self, rather than of the other. These different processes of differentiation may also be facilitated by the mother, who, identifying with their daughters more strongly, may have difficulty separating from them, whereas they may more easily push their sons away from them, or allow them to pull away (as also suggested by Chodorow).

According to Benjamin (1988), men develop a sexual subjectivity based on masculinity, and women develop a lack of sexual subjectivity. As Benjamin sums up: "man expresses desire and woman is the object of it" (p. 86). She argues that a woman's lack of sexual subjectivity is not due to her perceived biological lack of the penis which men possess (as per Freud's Oedipus model), but rather as arising out of "the totality of a girl's relationship with the father, in a context of gender polarity and unequal responsibility for child-rearing" (p. 86). As outlined above, Benjamin shows that for women and for men, the differentiation of self from other, the acquired assumptions about gender, and the conflicts that this evokes, occur long before the stage of the Oedipus complex.

According to Benjamin, the mother (and woman), although associated with fertility, is a desexualised figure. She argues that even the liberated, contemporary, 'sexy' woman, who has been loosened in her association to motherhood as womanhood, is not a sexual *subject*, but rather a sexual *object*. She is 'sexy' because of "her capacity to evoke desire in the other" (1988, p. 89). The woman, lacking desire of her own, thus must rely on the desire of the man. For Freud this was formulated through the notion of penis envy. However, Benjamin argues that this is not solely based on biology, but is also a social and cultural arrangement, and so it is not inevitable (as Freud would suggest). Rather, she interprets penis envy "as an expression of the girl's efforts to identify with the father as a way of establishing the separateness that is threatened by identifying with the mother" (p. 95). It is the father, not his phallus, that is the location of power and becomes an important other to help in the girl's battle to differentiate herself from mother.

The father represents for both the boy and the girl an exciting figure that represents the outside world of the mother, with whom they can also identify. Identifying with the father helps the child separate from the engulfing mother. The father is also the symbolic figure who 'owns' desire; the father is the subject of desire, while the mother is the object of desire (1988, p. 104). The mutual recognition between father and son allows the boy to identify with the father and to also become the subject of desire, and mother is retained as the object of desire. Benjamin shows how culturally this is also supported with common utterances like mother describing her son as her 'little man', for example. The father also tends to recognise himself in his son. For the girl, this experience with the father is different. The girl also wants to identify with the father so as to help her differentiate from her mother, but the father does not see himself in his daughter, and, furthermore, his own childhood disidentification with his mother and his need to assert his difference to women "make it difficult for him to recognise his daughter as he does his son" (p. 109). The distance in recognition she experiences with her father thus pushes the girl to turn back to her mother. She cannot identify with father's desire, and so she remains a sexual object, not a sexual subject, and in adulthood wants to have the father that she cannot be (p. 110). This relates to the ideas of Irene Fast on gender differentiation, discussed in Chapter 4.

Benjamin (1988) acknowledges that some feminist theorists would critique her repeating a description of women and of femininity as having a 'lack' in terms of sexual subjectivity, a lack of desire and their submissiveness. But she states how she does not describe these as inherent qualities of women. Rather, she writes about this as it reflects the reality of female subjectivity as it typically exists in our society and culture. Importantly though, she does not see this as innate, biological, or fixed; with changed experiences of mutual recognition, things can be different. As she later states in describing an intersubjective perspective, there is the potential for "a symmetry between two active partners" (1998, pp. 39–40), which changes traditional ideas about passivity and activity as equated with femininity and masculinity. Benjamin (1998), like Aron (1995), argues there to be a multiplicity of gender; we are all a bit masculine and a bit feminine, a bit active and a bit passive. In the Oedipal phase, gender complementarity "becomes an organising principle" and is "internalized as an ideal" (Benjamin, 1998, p. 66), although such complementarity does not necessarily determine heterosexuality. Benjamin agrees with Aron in emphasising that in the Oedipal triangular situation, the important achievement is the recognition that the two parental objects are separate and differentiated, and consequently, for the individual to be able "to imagine the partner as separate or different" (1998, p. 68).

The Oedipus Complex as a Model of Triangular Relationships

As introduced in Chapter 3, Klein's object relational model, and later developments by contemporary Kleinians, in particular Britton, have been influential in considering a more relational understanding of the Oedipus complex as a model of triangulated relationships between parent and child, such as that outlined by Aron (also discussed in Chapter 3). Here I will present the contributions from three further relational theorists: Hans Loewald, Thomas Ogden and Jody Messler Davies.

From Two-Person Relationship to Triangular Relationships

In his paper, *The Waning of the Oedipus Complex*, Loewald (1979) defines the Oedipus complex as the "psychic representation of a central, instinctually motivated, triangular conflictual constellation of child–parent relations" (pp. 751–752). He regards it as a stage of transition from the child's non-differentiated subject–object relationship to a triadic relationship with whole, separate objects; a stage involving the development of a self and entry into adulthood (Loewald, 1985).

Loewald critiques Freud's suggestion that the Oedipus complex of infantile sexuality is repressed and destroyed before the development of genital sexuality in adolescence. He suggests that the infantile Oedipus complex is never completely repressed or destroyed, and it is never fully resolved. Rather, it wanes (i.e. becomes progressively diminished), making its reappearance at various times in adolescence and adulthood, as the individual develops a growing independence and autonomy from his or her parents, and an adult sexual relationship of their own. This involves usurping the authority and power of the parents of infancy and childhood and relinquishing the incestuous libidinal investments in them. He argues that in the process of individuation, the partial 'killing off' (parricide) of one's parents of childhood is "a developmental necessity" (p. 759). How this developmental process proceeds partly depends on how parents react to their child's growing independence. Conflicts of this sort are observed in the various generational struggles. As Loewald states:

> In an important sense, by evolving our own autonomy, our own superego, and by engaging in nonincestuous object relations, we are killing our parents. We are usurping their power, their competence, their responsibility for us, and we are abnegating, rejecting them as libidinal objects. In short, we destroy them in regard to some of their qualities hitherto most vital to us. Parents resist as well as promote such destruction no less ambivalently than children carry it out. What will be left if things go well is tenderness, mutual trust, and respect – the signs of equality.
>
> (1979, p. 758)

With his focus on 'parricide', Loewald is referring to the authority of both parents in childhood. It is not only the father that is a figure of authority. He regards this as a necessary aspect of how a new generation comes to take over from the previous generation. However, the incestuous Oedipal currents also play a part in that it is not just a matter of 'destroying' what the previous generation has created, but to also build on it and transform it.

For Loewald, resolving the Oedipal complex requires some form of reconciliation of conflicting wishes and desires. Aggressive wishes are involved in the child's desire to become autonomous and independent, while incestuous wishes pull the child towards preserving unity with them. Loewald emphasises integration over repression. Rather than seeing the Oedipus complex as constituting forbidden desires and rivalrous wishes that need to be repressed, he perceives it as an essential phase wherein the child integrates external realities into their internal psychic world. This partly involves the internalisation of one's parents, which he describes as a form of atonement for the act of parricide. This integration helps the child navigate interpersonal relationships, gain independence from their parents, and gives them a sense of their own place in the wider world.

The Transitional Oedipal Relationship

Thomas Ogden (1989) provides some elaboration of the developmental move from a dyadic parent–child relationship to the triangular Oedipal relationship. He combines Freud's ideas of the Oedipus complex with the ideas of Klein and British Object Relations. He focuses on the interpersonal, psychological processes that mediate a child's transition into the Oedipus complex. Ogden takes more of a relational approach, in that when talking about object relations, he is not just considering the individual's relationship to internal objects (as would Klein), but to both the internal and external object (as did Winnicott). Ogden observes that as an individual moves into the depressive position, and develops the capacity to symbolise, one enters "the world of whole object relations", which he describes as follows:

> As one becomes capable of experiencing oneself as a subject, one at the same time (via projection and identification) becomes capable of experiencing one's "objects" as also being subjects. That is, other people are viewed as being alive and capable of thinking and feeling in the same way that one experiences oneself as having one's own thoughts and feeling.
>
> (1989, p. 12)

Ogden argues that the conflicts of the Oedipal complex are dilemmas "rooted in subjectivity" (p. 28). For example, the boy's hatred for the rival father can only really have intensity if there are also feelings of love for him. However, these conflicts become experienced mostly in paranoid-schizoid modes of experience. As previously noted in Chapter 3, the depressive position and the paranoid-schizoid position are always in interaction with one another.

Ogden develops the concept of a 'transitional Oedipal relationship' that the girl or boy has with their mother. This transitional Oedipal relationship is the period between the dyadic relationship of child–mother in the pre-Oedipal period, and the triadic relationship of the Oedipus complex. During the transitional Oedipal relationship, the child comes to gradually discover otherness. Ogden develops this idea from Winnicott's (1953) notion of the transitional object and transitional space, and how the external object is discovered through a gradual process of the disillusionment of omnipotent object relationship. The infant at first has a relationship to a 'subjective object' (the mother, the breast), which is experienced as part of the self. The child discovers external objects and external reality through the gradual mediation provided by the mother, for example through the process of weaning, and the use of a dummy as a transitional object. For Ogden, the child's entry into the Oedipus complex is one such process of transition from a subjective object to an external object.

In terms of the girl's transition into the Oedipus complex, Ogden suggests that the girl's switch in object of desire from mother to father is not explained by an innate heterosexuality, as others have previously argued (e.g. Chasseguet-Smirgel, Horney), nor as motivated by castration anxiety (as suggested by Freud). For Ogden, the switch is not from the object of mother to object of father, but rather a switch from

> a relationship to an internal object (an object that is not completely separate from oneself) to a cathexis of an external object (an object that exists outside of one's omnipotence). The external object encountered is not only the Oedipal father, but also the Oedipal mother with whom the Oedipal father has a relationship.
>
> (p. 112)

In a transitional Oedipal relationship, the girl is in love with her mother, who in her own unconscious is identified with her own Oedipal father, the 'father-in-mother'. Balsam (2015) suggests that this 'father-in-mother' is communicated to the daughter in her administrations of care. This is similar to the enigmatic messages that Laplanche speaks of (Chapter 5). Thus, in the context of a mother–daughter relationship, the girl also discovers and encounters the father, the representative of otherness, in the mother, through her externality. The mother unconsciously gives 'permission' for this discovery of separateness and otherness. This provides the girl with an introduction to a form of otherness which is also experienced as 'not-other' as it is within the subjective object relation with the mother (p. 118). As Ogden states: "the first heterosexual love relationship unfolds in the context of a relationship involving two females; the initial triangulation of object relations occurs within a dyadic relationship" (p. 6).

This transitional Oedipal relationship is experienced in part like a betrayal and a disillusionment by mother of the previous subjective object relationship. Gradually the child comes to discover both mother and father as separate, external objects, with the triangular relationships that this brings. Ogden argues that the hostile feelings towards the mother are not because of blaming her for her castration (as Freud formulated it), but rather out of feelings of betrayal for having an external life of her own. However, because of the nature of the transitional Oedipal relationship, this is not traumatic, as the relationship with the mother also embodies a relationship to the father in her unconscious: "*the little girl falls in love with mother-as-father and with the father-as-mother*" (p. 119 italics in the original). This links with the thoughts of André Green who states that there is always a representation of the father in the mother's unconscious mind, and so there is never *just* a mother–infant relationship (see Chapter 5). Where the mother is not able to provide this transitional Oedipal relationship, for example by seeming to forbid love of father or other men, or where the mother has her own unresolved Oedipal conflicts in her own unconscious, this will lead to Oedipal conflicts and problems for the girl. Ogden suggests that in the case of homosexuality, in the Oedipus complex the girl has love for her mother in the form of a sexual attachment of one female for another. The father is experienced with some ambivalence as the rival.

During the boy's transitional Oedipal relationship, the mother is both the internal maternal object and the external object of father (as he is present in her unconscious). However, the transition into the Oedipal complex for the boy differs as (in the case of hetero-sexuality) there is no change of object. The mother is both the internal omnipotent object of the pre-Oedipal period and the external whole object that is desired: "the Oedipal mother is and is not the same mother the little boy loved, hated, and feared prior to his discovery of her (and his father) as external Oedipal objects" (p. 142). There is a "psychological proximity" (p. 142) between the pre-Oedipal mother and Oedipal object of love. This creates some conflict for the boy, who takes on an object of love (a female other) which has links to the pre-Oedipal object that he experienced as partly undifferentiated from himself and with whom he had an omnipotent relationship, and from whom he needs to create distance. This conflict, Ogden states, is resolved through a set of primal scene phantasies, that creates a triangular dynamic between mother, child, and the third other, and organises sexual meanings and the boy's sense of himself. In this space of thirdness, the child discovers biological sexual difference and gen-erational difference. Primal scene phantasies are at first akin to the combined parent figure described by Klein of the paranoid-schi-zoid position. Here, the boy, in his undifferentiated state with the objects, is *part of the scene* (p. 149; italics in original). In the Oedipus complex, the boy's primal scene phantasies involve a more mature narrative of the external mother and external father in sexual intercourse.

According to Ogden, the little boy discovers "phallic thirdness" during the transitional Oedipal relationship with his mother, because her Oedipal father is in her unconscious mind, and this is brought into the relationship with the boy. The mother is experi-enced as both "father-in-mother and mother-in-father" (p. 153). As the boy enters the Oedipus complex, mother is increasingly perceived as a separate external object, as is the father, and they are observed as being a parental couple. Sex and generational difference can now be observed and acknowledged. The boy now can experience his own phallic sexual excitement, and identifying with the father, takes on the mother as the object of desire. As he is now the observer of the primal scene, rather than being a part of it, he is sufficiently separated from the dangers of incest (p. 155).

Considering Oedipal Complexity

Davies (2003) too takes a relational perspective on the Oedipus complex, arguing that parents participate in the Oedipal dynamics of their child. She points out how in Loewald's formulation of the child's act of symbolic parricide, the parents must be willing to be symbolically destroyed, and to be replaced as Oedipal love-objects. She places emphasis on a developmental shift from what she described as the incestuous object relations of the Oedipal experience to the development of post-Oedipal non-incestuous object relations. Rather than focusing on the particularities of object choice and sexual orientation, she emphasises the development of qualities of intimacy, eroticism, and mutuality, and the capacity to tolerate ambivalent and conflicting feelings within a loving relationship (p. 7). This development shift is influenced by the varieties of forms of emotional and relational engagement and disengagement between parent and child. As she describes:

> the oedipal love affair between parent and child is a deeply mutual, intensely romantic, and idealizing drama of erotic participation and parricide; one that must be entered into and lived out by both participants; and one that must be relinquished and mourned in equal measure by each participant as well.
>
> (p. 9)

The child must come to terms with the experience of being excluded from the parental couple, and the parent must come to terms with relinquishing their child as an idealised product, or extension, of themselves. The child must come to accept their own and their parent's limitations, and the parent must come to accept their child's and their own limitations. Thus, according to Davies, the Oedipal experience does not just involve the child having to relinquish their omnipotent and incestuous fantasies; the parents must also relinquish their idealised and 'romantic' fantasies about their child. For Davies, as for Loewald, the Oedipus complex is never resolved, as such struggles and dynamics wax and wane throughout childhood and adulthood.

Davies (2015) later referred to the need to consider the Oedipus complex in terms of "Oedipal complexity" (p. 256), which takes into account multiple heteroerotic and homoerotic currents between parent and child, and the parent's own emotional response to them. Thinking in this way facilitates a more nuanced consideration and understanding of an individual's unique "erotic signature" (p. 269). Davies suggestion of thinking about Oedipal complexity in relation to understanding sexual diversity will be revisited in Chapter 7.

Oedipal Complexity in the Film All of Us Strangers

The Oedipal complexity that Davies speaks of is effectively depicted in the 2023 film *All of Us Strangers* (directed by Andrew Haigh). The movie portrays the story of Adam, a gay man in his late 40s, and his encounters with the ghosts of his parents, who had died in a car crash in the mid-1980s, when he was 11 years old. The encounters with the ghosts of his parents represent memories of his childhood, and his parent's past homophobic attitudes, but also represent his relationship with them as internalised objects and internalised parental couple.

In the film, we are shown Adam's conflicting feelings of love (desire) and hostility and resentment towards both his mother and his father. Although his homoerotic desires towards his father are apparently stronger, his heteroerotic desires for his mother are also evident. We see the childhood wishes of wanting to possess each parent. His parents both kiss Adam on the mouth. He looks longingly at his father. He gets into the bed between them, having an intimate conversation with his mother. In the film this is filmed as Adam the adult but portrays his childhood desires and fantasies.

Part of the dynamic and the conflicts, however, involve the Oedipal complexities of his parents. His father comes across as homophobic and rejecting of his son's sexuality. However, in one scene when him and Adam are alone, talking about their past relationship, his father puts on a record (vinyl) and plays the love song "I Don't Want to Set the World on Fire", by the Ink Spots – "I just want to be the one you love", sings the lead singer. Adam's father says how it used to be his father's favourite, a reference perhaps to his own love for his father. So, we have Adam's father's own conflicting heteroerotic and possible homoerotic Oedipal feelings. More clearly depicted is Adam's mother's Oedipal complex. In one scene, Adam is caught in the rain and his clothes are soaked. His mother instructs him to take his wet clothes off, so she can put them to dry (as she would have when he was just a boy). He does so, embarrassed to undress to his underwear in front of her. She suddenly now sees him as an adult man, and comments on his adult masculine body. She comments on his hairless chest: "I thought you would be hairier, like your dad. I like a hairy chest myself", she says. And as she looks at him, she says how Adam reminds her of her own father. Depicted here is her own hetero-erotic Oedipal desires. Later, when Adam tells her that he is gay, she seems hurt and rejected by him, and Adam feels guilty as well as angry. The movie depicts how some of these Oedipal complex-ities are resolved, and how his parental objects become more benign, observing internalised figures (see Rohleder, 2025 for a more detailed analysis of the film).

Chapter 7

Challenging Heteronormativity

Psychoanalysis has a troubling history in its understanding of homosexuality (see Lewes, 1988; O'Connor & Ryan, 1993; also, Hertzmann & Newbigin, 2023). Heterosexuality was generally seen as the 'healthy', biologically pre-determined norm. This will have been evident in some of the theories discussed in earlier chapters. In this chapter I will discuss some of the attempts to challenge heteronormative accounts of the Oedipus complex that allows for a positive view of same-sex desire and object choice. There is a large body of literature from disciplines other than psychoanalysis that have been influential in challenging heteronormativity, such as Queer theory. It is beyond the scope of this introductory text to consider this body of work. However, I will begin with a brief acknowledgment of the influence of Queer theory. For the most part, I will consider psychoanalytic writing on the Oedipus complex and same-sex desire, firstly looking at reformulations of the Oedipus complex for male homosexuality, and then discussing approaches that have expanded on Freud's notion of innate bisexuality and adult sexual diversity. Finally, I will briefly discuss some studies that have looked at Oedipal dynamics in same-sex families.

Queering Sexuality and Gender

Much of the difficulty in psychoanalytic theories of the Oedipus complex has been the use of the gender binaries of male–female, masculine–feminine, and active–passive. These have been used as

DOI: 10.4324/9781003394471-7

"organising concepts" (Schafer, 2002) that maintain a hetero-normative framework for understanding human sexuality. Under this heteronormative framework, a man's desire and love for another man was typically understood as the man taking up a 'passive', 'feminine' position, and a woman's desire and love for another woman, as her taking up an 'active', 'masculine' position. Historically, in much of psychoanalytic theorising, it was under-stood that an individual could not identify with and at the same time desire an object of the same sex (O'Connor & Ryan, 1993). Typically, same-sex desire was seldom understood and theorised to be perceived in positive ways.

Queer theorists have challenged essentialist notions of gender and of sexuality, and the boundaries between 'masculine' and 'feminine', 'active' and 'passive', and heterosexual' and 'homo-sexual'. Queer theory emphasises the fluidity of gender and sexual identity. For example, the influential Queer studies theorist, Judith Butler (1990), understands gender to be socially constructed rather than biologically determined. Masculinity and femininity are 'performed'; that is, we differentiate between activities that are constructed as 'masculine' and activities that are constructed as 'feminine'. Butler also argues how 'heterosexuality' is dependent on the 'foreclosure' and disavowal of homosexual desire. Sexuality and gender are not biologically determined. This was a position sometimes taken up by Freud in some of his writing, however much of psychoanalytic theory tended to organise sexuality and gender in more heteronormative terms.

Queer theory has generally not been welcomed in psychoanalysis. In psychoanalytic theory, homosexuality has, for the most part, been perceived "as threatening a known certainty – the binary (masculine–feminine) heterosexual gender arrangement" (Corbett, 1993, p. 345), which Queer theory seeks to disrupt. However, in contemporary psychoanalysis this has changed. Among psycho-analytic theorists, Benjamin (1988) suggests that a psychologically 'healthy' individual is able to integrate both 'masculine' and 'femi-nine' aspects of self and be able to express these; Harris (2009) has argued that gender is 'softly assembled', with no particular outcome or identification being predictable. Others have argued that gender is multiple and creative, but subject to global regularities (Aron,

1995; Corbett, 2008). The reality is that we do not just identify with one parent. We identify with both. They in turn have identified with both. We have a mixture of what we may term 'masculine' and 'feminine' traits. When it comes to sexuality and sex, we are often also a mixture of 'active' and 'passive', and there exists homoerotic and heteroerotic currents. There may typically be more dominance of one over the other, or greater strength of identification of one over the other.

We might say that Queer theory has articulated the 'disorientated' and 'disorganised' nature of sexuality, and counter to this, the Oedipus complex, in much of 'traditional' psychoanalytic approaches, has tended to orientate and organise sexuality. Thus, in Queer theory, the Oedipus complex is often critiqued as to its real usefulness for understanding sexuality. For a rich, contemporary encounter between Queer theory and psychoanalysis, see Giffney and Watson (2017). For the remainder of this chapter, I focus on reformulations of the Oedipus complex that account for a 'positive' inclusion of, and development of, same-sex desire.

Reformulations of the Oedipus Complex and Male Homosexuality

Part of the problem in psychoanalytic theorising of the past was that openly gay men and lesbian women were mostly barred from psychoanalytic training. So, while there were many female psychoanalysts who were able to bring a feminist perspective on early psychoanalytic theories, there were no perspectives from gay psychoanalysts. Two important early contributions from openly gay clinicians came from Kenneth Lewes and Richard Isay.

Lewes' Re-Examination of the Oedipus Complex for Male Homosexuality

Lewes's book *The Psychoanalytic Theory of Male Homosexuality* (1988) provided an important examination of historic problematic and homophobic attitudes in psychoanalytic theorising on male homosexuality, and the gradual shifts to more humane perspectives. In the book, he also considers Freud's notion of innate bisexuality and the complete Oedipus complex. He outlines a "fourfold", "fully elaborated" Oedipus complex (p. 80). This fourfold complex includes the observation that the male child has ambivalent feelings towards both parents, with libidinal ties and rivalrous feelings to both his mother and his father. The mother or the father are both possible future object choices. He further distinguishes between the pre-Oedipal mother who is perceived as having a phallus, and the castrated mother of the Oedipal phase. The child may thus identify with the father and take a masculine gender identity, or with the phallic pre-Oedipal mother or the castrated mother and take a more feminine identity. The possible outcomes of the Oedipus complex depend on these varying bisexual components, as well as the intensity of heterosexual or homosexual libidinal attachments, whether there is a predominantly active or predominantly passive libidinal stance, and whether there is an anaclitic object choice (that is one based on a strong libidinal tie) or a narcissistic object choice. Lewes states that "there is no straight line from preoedipal constitution to postoedipal result" (1988, p. 82). The child can adopt one of a possible four objects (father, phallic mother, castrated mother, or self), and make one out of a possible three identifications (active masculine, active feminine, or passive feminine). This results in a total of 12 possible outcomes of the Oedipus complex, six of which Lewes categorises as heterosexual and six as homosexual. Here, Lewes retains some of the heteronormative organising aspects of Freud's theory of the Oedipus complex; however, homosexuality is also considered as an equally possible 'healthy' outcome.

Lewes (1998) later proposed the plicate, or 'folded', Oedipus complex as an alternative model for some homosexual men. He argues that some homosexual men (not all) experience the father as the sole object of libidinal desire during the phallic stage of psychosexual development, which Lewes argued begins at the start of the phallic stage, not at its end as Freud suggested. This homosexual desire for the father is biologically influenced. In this 'folded' Oedipus complex, the father occupies a paradoxical dual role: both the "exciter and the prohibitor of erotic arousal" (p. 347). This means the boy experiences desire for the father while simultaneously perceiving him as the source of prohibition and castration threat. This differs from the traditional model of the Oedipus complex, where these roles are typically split between the two parents. Although the plicate Oedipus complex involves only the father and son, Lewes considers it triadic because of the father's dual role. This triadic interaction is crucial because it establishes the father as a separate entity, independent of the son's desires, unlike the dyadic, need-gratifying relationship found in earlier stages of development.

Lewes contends that in the plicate Oedipus complex, the father's rejection of the son's advances stems from his preference for other erotic ties, often with the mother or sisters. This leads to the realisation for the son: "I love him, but he prefers her to me" (p. 352). This realisation underscores the father's separate existence, an important aspect of this model. The internalised castration threat, originating from the father in this case, necessitates repression fuelled by the son's own inhibitions, like guilt and fear.

Isay and Primary Homosexual Desire

Isay (1986) provided another reformulation of Freud's theory of the Oedipus complex, which has been frequently cited. He proposed a model of homosexual identity formation with three stages: childhood acquisition, adolescent and early adulthood consolidation, and adulthood integration. This model posits that homoerotic fantasies and impulses emerge in early childhood, from the ages of three through to five. Isay regards this period as comparable to the Oedipal stage of heterosexual boys, but with the father as the primary sexual object for the gay boy. He understood these homoerotic Oedipal feelings, not as a result of a defensive shift from the mother; rather, they are innate and contribute to the child's developing homosexual identity. These homoerotic fantasies are consolidated in adolescence, with the experience of masturbation to homoerotic fantasies, and homoerotic patterns of sexual arousal. However, due to feelings of shame and perceived social homophobic intolerance, these feelings are supressed and there is little overt homosexual activity. Isay distinguishes between the prevalence of experimental homoerotic 'play' sexual activity among some heterosexual boys, and the "for real", passionate homoerotic sexual arousal of the gay boy (1986,

p. 479). Gradually the gay adolescent comes to a stage of acceptance of their homosexuality usually in late adolescence or early
adulthood, with a more integrated sexual orientation having
developed. Isay (1987) also observed that some gay boys adopt
opposite-sex characteristics in childhood, not to appease the father
but to gain his love and attention. According to Isay, this suggests
that the child's innate attraction to the father, a key aspect of the
Oedipus complex for gay men, precedes and influences their
behaviour and identification, rather than the other way around.

Goldsmith (1995, 2001) extends the work of Isay to propose a
distinct Oedipal stage, or "developmental pathway" (1995, p. 112),
specific to gay boys where the father is the primary love object,
and the mother becomes the rival for his affection. Goldsmith
likens this dynamic to the Greek myth of Orestes, who kills his
mother to avenge the death of his father. Gay boys face the challenge of managing not only their erotic feelings for their fathers
but also their anger and aggression towards their mothers, cou-
pled with a fear of their mothers' potential retaliation. He argues
that this Oedipal dynamic, with the father as the primary love
object, is the dominant experience for homosexual boys, shaping
their psychosexual development, unlike heterosexual boys for
whom the 'negative' Oedipal complex is secondary.

Goldsmith further observes the societal expectation that children will form a 'childhood romance' with their opposite-sex
parent. This is evident in common expressions like 'daddy's little
girl' and 'mommy's little boy'. Similarly, competition and emula-
tion of the same-sex parent are implicitly and explicitly endorsed
for heterosexual children. However, for gay boys, this societal
norm creates a challenge, as their internal experiences contrast
with parental and social expectations. Both Isay and Goldsmith
argue that the gay child's longing for the father may be met with
withdrawal or rejection from fathers who, sensing their son's 'difference', are either unable or unwilling to reciprocate their son's
feelings. Goldsmith further observes that societal expectation of a
'childhood romance' with the mother can be particularly challenging for gay boys who may harbour competitive and aggressive
feelings towards them. Goldsmith explains that mothers, often
anticipating this 'childhood romance', may unwittingly exacerbate

these feelings through their affection, creating a distorted perception of their mothers as intrusive, seductive or aggressive, partly a projection of his own rivalrous feelings towards her for their father's affection. Thus, Isay and Goldsmith reformulate previous pathologising formulations of male homosexuality being 'caused by' distant fathers and over-bearing or dominant mothers, arguing instead that fathers may become distant, and mothers be perceived as over-bearing in response to the child's emerging homosexuality. Goldsmith suggests that this misaligned Oedipal drama makes it difficult for homosexual boys to openly express their feelings out of fear of rejection, and so their true feelings are neither acknowledged nor reciprocated.

Case Study: 'Jacob'

This case study has been previously published (Rohleder, 2020, pp. 52–53) and is reproduced here with permission. I have made minor amendments, in part to fit the material more with the content and discussion of this chapter.

Jacob was a gay man in his late 20s who sought psychotherapy at the suggestion of his HIV clinician, as he was struggling with loneliness and "rejection issues" related to his HIV status. He also had a history of self-destructive behaviour (binge drinking, previous drug use, and frequent casual sex). In my first session with him, he said that previous bouts of "binge sex" were prompted by feelings of loneliness and frustration. Since his HIV diagnosis (less than a year previously), he was trying to live a healthy life, and had controlled his drinking, stopped taking drugs, and stopped "binge sex". It became apparent that his HIV diagnosis weighed heavily on him, and that he thought of it as a "punishment" which he "deserved".

Jacob described being close to his mother. However, she seemed to have had emotional difficulties, as a result of traumatic life events of her own. He said how she could quite often be "needy" and "emotional", turning to him for support. He was not close to his father or his younger brother. He described his father as "emotionally cold" and verbally aggressive. He said he had "nothing in common" with him and had grown up feeling "different". Although the eldest, he said that "I was never the prized son that my brother was". In contrast, he felt that he was "pushed away" by his father. He described his childhood and adolescence as difficult, that he was teased and bullied by his peers for being effeminate. His first gay sexual relationship was with a man some years older. They lived together for four years, but Jacob had difficulties with intimacy and was always jealous and insecure with his boyfriend, suspecting him of having affairs. Around the time of starting therapy, he had met and begun a relationship with a new man, and the relationship, as with the previous one, soon ran into difficulties. Jacob was insecure and easily got angry, leading to frequent arguments.

Initially my work with Jacob was set up as time-limited psychotherapy in the context of his HIV diagnosis. Recognising some of his long-standing difficulties, we soon discussed the possibility of ongoing work. However, almost from the start, Jacob felt insecure with me. He found the space beneficial, and he recognised his need to work through things, but he was ambivalent about whether he should come for more or not. He started to miss sessions, questioning, with some anger, whether he needed psychotherapy. The sessions started to feel a little chaotic, with Jacob denigrating therapy, but at the same time seeming to need it. I was left feeling unsure whether he would stay or go. In one session he talked about his frustration at work (in a hotel), complaining that the managers were "cold" towards the kitchen and cleaning staff whom Jacob saw as "desperate", poor, and in need of help. It was not a stretch to suggest to him that he was talking about his own desperate need for help, but his fear that I would find him unacceptable, and reject and humiliate him. Eventually he agreed to come for ongoing psychotherapy but warned me of his "badness" to come. I interpreted that he longed for a relationship but was aware of the anger that disguised a damaged, ashamed part of himself, which he did not want others to see.

During one session, after some months, he was talking about his struggles with HIV, his fear and his loneliness. He was very tearful in the session, saying "this is not how I imagined my life would turn out to be". When I announced the end of the session, he became angry that we could not continue, asking whether I had another patient after him. Two days later he called me, leaving a voice mail to say that he had paid his outstanding bill into my bank account and confirmed his next appointment. At this next session, we spoke of how angry he had felt when I turned him away at the end of the previous session. He said how he had wondered whether he should "fire his therapist". I acknowledged his anger and sense of rejection and his wish to make me the rejected one. I interpreted his phone call as his checking to see if I was still OK; that his rage had not damaged me. He then proceeded to talk about his adolescence and the build-up to his coming out at age 17. Struggling to talk through tears, he spoke about how he was "treated like a disease" by his father and brother, and his peers.

Jacob's desire for intimacy but fear of rejection reflect the sort of Oedipal conflict described by Isay and Goldsmith. His Oedipal same-sex desire, fear of rejection and feelings of rivalry and hostility were alive in the transference with me. My suggestion of ongoing work was a move towards greater intimacy, which he found frightening. I was the desired object, but also the rejecting object, like his father. While experiencing closeness with his mother, his relationship to her was also fraught with ambivalence, experiencing her as intrusive, possibly a projection of his rivalrous feelings for the affection of his father. He felt a longing for intimacy, including with me, but I was also the enforcer that prohibited this desire (as proposed by Lewes), which he felt in my enforcing the boundary at the end of the session. He felt the rivalry with my other patient, which in his fantasy represented his father's / my preferred son. His conflicting feelings were also expressed in his calling me to say he had paid the bill, making loving reparation for his previously expressed aggression. The focus of the work with Jacob was not only to work with his feeling of shame and internalised homophobia, partly connected to his HIV, but also his Oedipal struggles of feelings of exclusion, envy and jealousy, and acceptance of his same-sex desire and wish for intimacy.

Psychic Bisexuality and Same-Sex Desire

Deborah Luepnitz (2019) argues that Freud's notion of innate bisexuality and the complete Oedipus complex was largely overlooked in favour of what she refers to as an 'Oedipus simplex' model that emphasised a heteronormative narrative. Several contemporary psychoanalysts have returned to Freud's conceptualisation of a complete Oedipus complex, highlighting heterosexuality, homosexuality, and bisexuality all as equally healthy possible sexual orientations.

Primary Femininity and Same-Sex Desire

Dianne Elise (2002) observed that in much of psychoanalytic writing, the development of female heterosexuality was by no means straightforward to formulate, whereas female homosexuality seems to be much easier to understand. Some of her work about the Oedipal development of boys and girls was discussed in Chapter 4. As previously mentioned, she suggests the term 'primary femininity' says more about a female's internalisations of social-cultural norms, rather than her sense of self and her body. A 'primary sense of femaleness' refers to the fact of biological sex, which differs to the development and expression of femininity, which is more socially and culturally shaped. However, as she states, "culture comes in quickly" (p. 491), and there is no real 'before' when it comes to the influence of social constructions of gender. For example, parents often make gendered decisions about the colour of baby clothes according to the sex of their baby. Nevertheless, Elise regards primary sense of femaleness and a sense of femininity as separate aspects of psychological development, which may align or not. An individual may have a sense of themselves as female with a female body, but not necessarily identify as feminine. She argues that the sense of being female can co-exist with the bisexual matrix and the fantasy of unlimited gender as explicated by Fast (discussed in Chapter 4). This in turn is distinct from sexual orientation. In other words, a woman may have a sense of themselves as female, and have various feminine and masculine identifications, and be lesbian.

Elise (2002) observes the important role played by the girl's early homosexual libidinal bond to her mother for her development. She states how "the girl's object relational constellation centrally involves the experience of homoeroticism as well as heteroeroticism" (p. 211). This primary homoerotic desire is the basis for the continuing development of homosexuality for some girls. However, the girl's homoerotic desire for her mother is often unregistered and unrecognised, in much the same way as Isay suggests the father might typically turn away from the homoerotic desire of his son. According to Elise (1997), underlying a sexual orientation are varying cross-sex and same-sex mental representations, not only of the self, but also of others. Thus, "multiple combinations exist intrapsychically that are not bound to the anatomical sex of the partners or to the core gender identity of either" (1997, p. 505).

Psychic Bisexuality and the Complete Oedipus Complex

Quite often when psychic bisexuality is considered in psychoanalysis it may tend to take a heteronormative form, in that this bisexuality gets organised into complimentary binaries that pair masculinity with femininity, which misses an opportunity for more nuanced and affirming thinking about same-sex desire and of bisexual orientation. Susann Heenen-Wolff (2011) and Deborah Luepnitz (2019, 2021) invite us to think about psychic bisexuality as the basis for the development of equally valid and 'healthy' homosexual and bisexual orientations.

Heenen-Wolff (2011) observes how a child at first is hardly cognisant or pays much attention to the sex of their primary object. The choice of object, she states, is tied to bodily experiences and varying individual and social factors. She argues that homosexuality and heterosexuality, and indeed adult bisexuality, must be understood as developing from primary bisexuality, with each being an equally valid orientation. She points out how in contemporary approaches we must think in terms of 'homosexualities', emphasising the variability of a person's sexuality. She further draws from Laplanche (discussed in Chapter 5), who suggested that the Oedipus complex acts as a meta-narrative that exists in the realm of the preconscious, to argue that "we only 'tell' ourselves that we are heterosexual or homosexual" (Heenen-Wolff, 2011, p. 1217), and that in the unconscious we are, and remain, bisexual. She concludes that we can't think of the 'healthy' resolution of the Oedipus complex in terms of heterosexuality, as previously asserted, but rather as involving the complete Oedipus complex. She states:

Infantile sexuality has not – yet – experienced a definitive object-choice and the heterosexual genital constellation is but *one* of the forms which infantile sexuality may arrive at, the 'polymorphic perverse' elements always remaining alive and active. This is why it is more appropriate to define the 'mature' psychic structure as a *potential* for the complete Oedipus complex and its 'dissolution', which is subject to updating throughout life.

(p. 1218)

Luepnitz (2019, 2021) argues for a 'reclaiming' of Freud's 'negative' Oedipus complex, and the use of the 'complete Oedipus complex' for providing a more comprehensive understanding of sexuality, regardless of an individual's sexual orientation. She prefers using the terms 'same-sex' and 'cross-sex' to describe the two sides of the Oedipus complex, instead of 'positive' and 'negative', which she acknowledges have strong value connotations and potential for pathologising. In the psychoanalysis of old, emphasis is typically placed on understanding homosexuality as a disinterest in, or anxious disavowal of, desire of the opposite sex, with little credence given to the real alive desire for the same sex. Thus, the use of the labels 'invert' or 'negative' focusing on what is absent, what is missing, rather than what is positively present. She suggests that a person's adult sexual orientation can be understood as the dominance of one or the other, or non-dominance of either: "adult heterosexual identity reflects a dominance of the cross-sex Oedipus, and homosexual identity a dominance of the same-sex, with bisexuality corresponding to a non-dominance of either" (2019, p. x). Luepnitz argues for the importance of considering and being attentive to both cross-sex and same-sex desires in all patients, to embrace the "Oedipal yarn" in all its entirety (2021, p. 629).

Thinking About 'Oedipal Complexity'

The conceptualisation of the complete Oedipus complex is developed further by some relational psychoanalysts, who have formulated the notion of "Oedipal complexity" (Davies, 2015 – discussed in Chapter 6). Davies redefines the Oedipus complex by challenging, and shifting away from, a linear heteronormative developmental theory of sexuality and sexual object choice. She argues that inherent bisexuality informs an individual's erotic imaginations, regardless of their sexual orientation. She suggests that every child develops both homoerotic and heteroerotic Oedipal configurations: "all of us must integrate the idealized and deidealized aspects of both heterosexual and homosexual incestuous engagements" (2003, p. 10), and that the capacity to do this is influenced by the responses of the child's parents. At worst, a child may be met with their parent's homophobic response, when they turn to the same-sex parent as an Oedipal love object, similar to the Oedipal rejection described by Isay and described in the case study of Jacob.

Davies's perspective contrasts with Freud, who saw bisexuality as a "*developmentally* universal phenomenon" (Davies, 2015, p. 268; italics in original), with the 'negative' (or homoerotic) aspects of early sexuality eventually being outgrown. Davies posits that each child develops a primary and secondary Oedipal configuration. She defines primary Oedipal configurations as referring to erotic experiences related to the same-sex parent for individuals developing a homosexual orientation, or the opposite-sex parent for those developing a heterosexual orientation. Secondary Oedipal configuration refers to the erotic experiences with parents and significant others of the opposite sex to the primary configuration. For the individual with a homosexual orientation, this would be erotic experiences with the parent of the opposite sex. Rather than fixed, Davies regards these Oedipal configurations as fluid, that both primary and secondary Oedipal configurations, which are shaped by early interactions with parents and significant others, contribute to an individual's unique erotic signature, regardless of sexual orientation, shifting between foreground and background, unconscious and conscious, depending on the individual's relationships and experience. Difficulties in integrating primary and secondary Oedipal configurations can lead to inhibitions in erotic expression and the capacity for fulfilling romantic relationships. She suggests that the secondary configuration is often more conflictual and, therefore, more likely to be repressed or projected, making it less available to erotic imagination and sexual fantasy.

Thus, Davies sees the Oedipus complex as a multifaceted system of fantasies stemming from both homoerotic and heteroerotic self-object organisations. Davies believes it is not the choice of sexual object, but the capacity to sustain passion and eroticism in relationships, regardless of the object choice, that the Oedipal complex determines. Analysing both primary and secondary configurations can enhance an individual's understanding of their erotic selves and potentially lead to greater freedom and fulfilment in their relationships, regardless of sexual orientation.

The Oedipus Complex in Same-Sex Families

Research suggests that children of same-sex couples are not less psychologically 'healthy', and are subject to similar developmental Oedipal conflicts, than children of heterosexual parents (Eitan-Persico, 2024; Nathans, 2021). The typical triadic relational dynamics involving feelings of exclusion and inclusion, desire, jealousy, and rivalry have been observed in children of same-sex parents as well as in the parent–child dynamics of single-parent families (Nathans, 2021).

Ken Corbett (2001), following Aron (1995), critiques the heteronormative 'singularity' of the primal scene concept in much of psychoanalysis. He points out how heterosexuality tended to be symbolised as the core aspects of reality and the 'facts of life'. He points out that while most children are conceived through heterosexual intercourse and most children come to learn that babies are conceived that way, there also exists variance to this. Corbett includes "*technological* reproductive realities" (2001, p. 618; italics in original) in contemporary life. He suggests that we may consider the existence of two 'primal scenes' in the fantasies of children of same-sex couples, one involving fantasies about the biological couple, and the second involving fantasies about the couple who brought the child up.

Vittorio Lingiardi and Nicola Carone (2019) reconsider Freud's idea of the child's development of a 'family romance' during the Oedipal phase; that is a fantasy about not being the child of his or her parents, but rather of another, usually more prestigious, parent couple. Freud regarded the 'family romance' as a defensive fantasy, that split 'good' from 'bad', and allowed for expressions of differentiation or separation as well as attachment. In the case of same-sex families where the child is conceived through third-party reproduction (and also, for that matter, in heterosexual families where a donor was required to have a child), a possible 'family romance' involving another couple, partly exists in reality. Lingiardi and Carone argue that we might think of the 'family romance' in these cases, not as a defensive fantasy, but rather "as a relational mode for 'feeling at home' with the fantasies of origins", which allows for the working through of possible anxieties about donor or surrogate involvement (2019, p. 235).

Yifat Eitan-Persico (2024) has published results of his analysis from a psychoanalytic qualitative study exploring Oedipal dynamics and experiences in 33 same-sex families in Israel, where the same-sex parents had a child, aged between 4 and 6 at the time of the study, with the aid of third-party reproduction (an egg or sperm donor). In his analysis of the data, he shows the existence of Oedipal triangular relational dynamics that one would expect to observe in any family. There were dynamics involving a greater expressed desire towards one parent, with more rivalry towards another (in these families both parents being of the same sex). In addition to these, there were triangular dynamics involving the child, 'birth others', and the parental couple, and between the child, biological parent, and the non-biological parent. Not only for the children, but for the same-sex couple too. There were the expected conflicting feelings of desire and jealousy, feelings of inclusion and exclusion, perceived similarities and differences between the sexes. The complexities created by the presence of 'birth others' and the experience of homophobic prejudice that some of these families had to endure, meant that it was not always easy or straightforward for the children. Some struggled, but overall, there was no observable 'damaging' consequences for the children, as there might have been assumed to be in the past when homosexuality was more pathologised.

Chapter 8

Culture and the Oedipus Complex

The question is often posed: Is the Oedipus complex universal? There are two ways of considering this: whether it is experienced by everyone in their childhood development, or whether it is evolutionary and biologically inherited by everyone (that is whether it is phylogenetic). In *Totem and Taboo*, Freud claimed that the Oedipus complex has phylogenetic roots. This is, perhaps, what has been most contested. In this chapter I will briefly outline Freud's claims and discuss just two important published and often cited studies investigating this: the study by Bronislaw Malinowski and the rebuttal study by Melford Spiro. I will then briefly look at studies that compare other cultural myths to the Oedipus myth. Finally, I will provide a brief review of research that looks at some of the cross-cultural variations of the Oedipus complex.

The Oedipus Complex and Society

In *Totem and Taboo*, Freud (1913) set out to apply his psycho-analytic thought to anthropology and put forward his ideas about the establishment of civilisation and the cultural taboo against incest. In this work, Freud hypothesised that the dynamics of the Oedipus complex are phylogenetic, and universal. That is, castration anxiety and the enforcement of the incest taboo characteristic of the Oedipus complex is evolutionary and biologically inherited. Freud drew on the work of Darwin and Robertson Smith to consider the establishment of totemic society and the primal horde. The 'primal horde' referred to an archaic stage of human development characterised by

DOI: 10.4324/9781003394471-8

a hierarchical society ruled by the primal father, who held absolute authority and control over access to females, creating a system of sexual repression and intense rivalry among the younger males in the horde, some of whom were driven out from the horde. In retaliation, some of the sons initiated a collective rebellion against the tyrannical rule of the primal father and murdered him. Having killed the primal father and taken over control of the horde, the sons agreed to outlaw incest, so as to protect their bond, creating a totem clan and enforcing exogamy (the custom of marrying outside the clan or tribe). Additionally, their overwhelming feelings of guilt and remorse for having killed the once-loved primal father resulted in the prohibition of patricide. The gratification of instinctual aggressive wishes and the enforcement of patricide was achieved through the ritual of sacrifice of a totem animal, a symbol of the primal father. Freud summarises:

> They revoked their deed by forbidding the killing of the totem, the substitute for their father; and they renounced its fruits by resigning their claim to the women who had now been set free. They thus created out of their filial sense of guilt the two fundamental taboos of totemism, which for that very reason inevitably corresponded to the two repressed wishes of the Oedipus complex. Whoever contravened those taboos became guilty of the only two crimes with which primitive society concerned itself.
>
> (p. 143)

Freud thus regarded the original Oedipus complex of the primal horde as the source of civilisation, society, and culture. The Oedipus complex, with its component dispositions of castration anxiety and the incest taboo, is biologically inherited and exists as innate primal phantasies in the unconscious. Freud's formulation of the origins and universality of the incest taboo has been challenged by numerous anthropologists. It is beyond the scope of this chapter to examine the literature on this. Perelberg (2015) provides a useful brief overview of some of the key figures in the anthropology literature. One key writer is the anthropologist Claude Lévi-Strauss (1969), who argued that the incest taboo is not something that can be understood as determined within the biological family, but rather exists as a social and cultural structure. He argued that kinship structures are maintained in any society through the rules of marriage, which are created and maintained by the exchange of women. That is, men exchange women as objects of value in a kinship system. Fathers give their daughter's hand in marriage to a man from another family. Incest is prevented by offering a family's women to men from another family.

One important critique to Freud that is often cited came from Bronislaw Malinowski (1927/2001), who claimed to have provided evidence of a society in which there was no trace of the Oedipus complex, as formulated by Freud. Both the writing of Freud in *Totem and Taboo* and of Malinowski are a product of their time, with references made to 'civilised' society and 'savages' or 'uncivilised' society, which makes for some uncomfortable reading today.

The Oedipus Complex in the Trobriands

Malinowski, a Polish-British anthropologist and ethnologist, presented his findings and critique in his book *Sex and Repression in Savage Society* (1927/2001). In this book, he asks if the Oedipus complex, corresponding to the Christian "patrilineal Aryan family", also exists in "savage or barbarous society" (p. 6). To investigate this question, Malinowski sought to observe the matrilineal culture of the Trobriand Islanders of North-Eastern New Guinea and compare it with the patrilineal family of Freud's Europe. He offers a detailed account of his observations, and quite often, merely his opinions.

Malinowski describes how in the Trobriand culture, kinship is recognised through the mother only, with succession running through the females of the family. The male child follows the values and social status of the maternal uncle, and inherits from the maternal uncle or aunt, not the father. In traditional Trobriand beliefs, a man and woman marry, but the husband is not the recognised biological father of the children that are born. Rather, children are believed to be inserted into the womb of the mother by the ancestral spirits. The husband's role is to protect and look after the children, but they are not 'his' children. Thus, the father is not a recognised kinsman. The father provides loving care and support, but it is the maternal uncle who has any authority over the children. A strict taboo exists preventing any intimate relationship between brothers and sisters, with male children and female children kept separate in the family. The mother recognises and respects the authority of her brother. The father in turn exercises the same role for his sisters and his sisters' children.

In comparing the two cultures, Malinowski observes that both customs support the strengthening of the bond between the mother and child immediately after birth, and that for the infant there is the facilitation of a state of satisfaction and bliss. In the Trobriand culture, however, he observed the father having a much closer presence with the children, forming more affectionate ties with the infants than he observed in European culture. After weaning, the father in the European culture enjoys a patriarchal status. While still maintaining a relative distance to the children, as head of the family he begins to assert authority and discipline over the children. This results in a disruption to the early infantile harmony. In the Trobriand culture, by comparison, Malinowski observed a continuing harmony as the father continues in a loving and nurturing role, having no recognised authority over the children.

When it came to observed behaviours indicative of childhood sexuality, Malinowski recorded no indication of repression of the child's genital sexual behaviours, as would be observed by Freud in European society. Malinowski concluded that the early libidinal bliss or desire directed at the mother disappears after weening, rather than is repressed, as the father does not at this time intervene as an authoritative figure. The Oedipus complex for the child in the Trobriands develops at a later stage, and involves the boy's sister and uncle, rather than his mother and father. During the stage of latency and adolescence, children in the Trobriand culture are afforded more freedom of sexual expression, although a strict taboo against brother–sister incest is enforced. This sexual freedom has the effect of dissipating any of the libidinal feelings that the boy had towards the mother before then. Interesting to note is the observation from anthropology that historically across many cultures, children were exposed to 'the primal scene' and sex, in large part due to a lack of privacy in most homes which facilitated a sexual enlightenment among children. Concerns about the privacy of the primal scene and parent's sexuality, and the practice of having separate beds and rooms, are a "relatively modern cultural practice" (Josephs, 2011, p. 92). In many areas of poverty in contemporary society there is little privacy in the home.

In the Trobriand culture, the authority of the maternal uncle enters the male child's life at a later stage than the authority of the father is present in the life of the child in European culture. In the Trobriand context, the maternal uncle does not live with the nuclear family, at times living in a different village. Thus, his authority is exercised at a distance. He instils a set of values to the boy and is idealised as a figure who should be pleased. Malinowski argues that in the matrilineal society of Trobriand culture, social arrangements are in harmony with the biological course of development of the child, while in the patrilineal society of European culture, several natural sexual impulses are restricted and repressed, resulting in frictions between the father and child. As mentioned earlier, in the Trobriand society the taboo of incest is most strictly enforced between brother and sister, rather than with the mother. Malinowski concludes there to be a different Oedipal structure in the two cultures. He states:

> Applying to each society a terse, though somewhat crude formula, we might say that in the Oedipus complex there is the repressed desire to kill the father and marry the mother, while in the matrilineal society of the Trobriands the wish is to marry the sister and to kill the maternal uncle.
>
> (p. 64)

Important to note, though, that Malinowski describes here a triangular dynamic, just not the one Freud identified for the male child. By extrapolation to other 'non-Western' cultures, Malinowski concludes that the Oedipal complex, as formulated by Freud, is not universal, but rather particular to the social context. His study and critique was considered important and tended to influence anthropologists' argument that the Oedipus complex was not universal. Of course, it has also been met with numerous critiques. A substantial critique comes from Melford Spiro.

Spiro's Critique

Spiro, in his book *Oedipus in the Trobriands* (1982/2010), described Malinowski's study as flawed and its data as "frustratingly
thin" (p. 2) and concluded that it was a weak thesis on which to
base the claim that the Oedipus complex is not universal. In
examining the evidence provided by Malinowski, Spiro concludes
that it does not support his claim that the boy's libidinal desires
towards his mother disappears prior to the start of the Oedipus
complex. While there is a taboo against brother–sister incest,
Spiro suggests that there is evidence for a myth and taboo for
mother–son incest in Trobriand culture too. With regards Malinowski's claim of the boy's rivalrous hostility towards the uncle,
Spiro points out how no direct evidence is offered, it is merely
inferred. He goes on to show how Malinowski rejects the notion
of the father as an Oedipal rival because he holds no authority,
but does not consider the father as a rival for the libidinal feelings
the boy has towards his mother. Spiro points out how in Freud's
conceptualisation of the boy's Oedipus complex, it is not that the
boy loves his mother *and* hates his father as the authority figure,
which Spiro claims is what Malinowski bases his observations on,
but rather that the boy hates his father *because* he loves his
mother. His Oedipal rivalry with the father arises out of his desire
for his mother, in this triangular constellation. Spiro also points
out how Malinowski does not allow for the possibility that the
desire felt towards the mother is repressed out of fear of a powerful rival (whether it be from the father or the uncle), and Spiro
shows how the boy's father does indeed exercise some authority
over the boy in Trobriand society, much more authority than
Malinowski claimed. Drawing on additional observational data
from the Trobriands, not used by Malinowski, Spiro goes on to
argue that traces of the Oedipus complex as formulated by Freud
are evident in Trobriand culture; an unusually strong Oedipus
complex that exists in repressed form, evident in some of the
myths, and ceremonial customs.

In the final chapter of his book, Spiro goes on to review some of
the published studies examining the incest taboo and Oedipal
constellations that are drawn on to establish whether the Oedipus

complex is universal or not (I will not refer to those studies here. Readers can turn to Spiro's book for these). Spiro concludes that there is evidence for the universality of the Oedipus complex, although there are cross-cultural variations in terms of structure (e.g. adoptive parents rather than biological parents), intensity, and outcome. Spiro provides the following observations and conclusions:

> the evidence for the universality of a motivational disposition to mother–son incest… is very strong, and since (as we argued above) the existence of the incestuous dimension of the Oedipus complex renders its aggressive dimension all but axiomatic, the only appropriate response to the question, "Is the Oedipus complex universal?" is "How could it not be?"
>
> (p. 162)

While the universality of the incest taboo is well-supported, Freud's theory that the two core dispositions of the Oedipus complex, castration anxiety and the horror of incest, are biologically inherited and exist as innate primal phantasies is contested. Mark Solms (2021), a neuroscientist and psychoanalyst, argues that this would suggest the existence of inherited non-declarative episodic memories (that is memories of events that cannot be recalled), which he points out is neuroscientifically impossible, as "there is no such thing as non-declarative episodic memory" (p. 559). However, Solms puts forward a plausible argument for the biological origins of castration anxiety as a form of innate fear response that evolved by means of natural selection, where a behavioural disposition to avoid genital risk (particularly for males whose genitals are exposed) would increase reproductive success. Solms also offers a revised explanation for the biological origins of the Oedipus complex, which I will discuss in the final chapter.

Cross-Cultural 'Oedipal' Myths

Another method for considering the universality of the Oedipus complex is to look at myths from other cultures that may have parallels with the themes depicted in the Greek myth of Oedipus. I will touch on just a few that have been published in the psycho-analytic literature.

Hägglund and Hägglund (1981) explored Oedipal-related themes in Finish folklore, where they find stories of a boy who kills his father and marries his mother, but that also includes a clearer account of the parents' role in the dynamics, more so than the myth of Oedipus. This includes accounts of the father's envy towards his wife and her capacity for childbearing, which gets displaced as envy towards his son.

Sudhir Kakar (1989), writing about Oedipal dynamics in Indian culture, argues that the castration anxiety of the Oedipus complex is not centred so much on the fear of punishment, as is the case for Freud, but rather reflects the primitive fantasy of being a woman, reflected in myths of the maternal-feminine goddess, the goddess as mother, and the centrality of "maternal configurations" in Indian culture (p. 356). Kakar goes on to say that:

> The wish to be a woman is one particular solution to the dis-cord that threatens the breaking up of the son's fantasized connexion to the mother, a solution whose access to aware-ness is facilitated by the culture's views on sexual differentia-tion and the permeability of gender boundaries.
>
> (p. 358)

Tang and Smith (1996) compare three myths from different cul-tures: The Greek myth of Oedipus, the Chinese tale of Hsueh, and the Indian legend of Ganesa. All three myths concern the triadic relationship between child (son), mother, and father, with themes of incest taboo and murderous rivalry. However, they point out several differences; one key difference being that in the myth of Oedipus the act of parricide is performed, whereas in the stories of Hsueh and Ganesa infanticide occurs. They argue that this difference partly reflects differing cultural traditions of child-rearing, the nature of a son's relationship to his father, and the traditionally understood ways in which a boy becomes a man. In Western culture (story of Oedipus), this is reflected by the son's need to break away from father and mother in order to become an independent adult man (thus the act of parricide). In Indian culture (story of Ganesa),

Tang and Smith suggest that the son is allowed by his father to become an independent adult. In Chinese culture (story of Hsueh) a son is expected to remain a filial son, to obey and respect the father as elder authority. However, the Oedipus myth doesn't only depict a tale of parricide; remember that in the story, Laius and Jocasta initially order the infant Oedipus to be killed (see Chapter 1). Tang and Smith consider that the role of the women in these three stories may also reflect cultural differences in how women are perceived, with women in Chinese culture perceived as less threatening, in Indian culture as limited in their power, and in Greek culture as more powerful, seductive figures.

Ming Dong Gu (2006) notes how the Oedipus complex narrative or key Oedipal themes do not typically feature in traditional Chinese literature. Gu argues that this is owing to the much greater degree of emotional repression owing to systematised moral and ethical codes in Chinese culture. He argues that in 'Western' cultures, families are typically focused on the individual as relatively independent, while the Chinese family can be described as "heavily collectively centred" (p. 166), with individual needs and interests sacrificed for the interests of the family. Gu suggests that, rather than the appearance in Chinese literature of Oedipus complex narrative in its nuclear form (involving mother, father, and child), it appears in fragmented, multiple "individual complexes" (p. 167). There is the 'father complex', which is the father's fear of his son as a rival figure (as depicted in the Oedipus myth). Then there is the 'mother complex' that in the Oedipus myth is depicted by Jocasta taking on Oedipus as a substitute for her lost husband. The 'mother complex' may also be reflected in a mother's jealousy towards her son's wife, who is seen as taking her son away from her. The 'son complex', is depicted in Chinese literature as the son's Oedipal feelings being repressed and becoming expressed in other forms, particularly a young man's longing for "a woman who has a mother stature or is a surrogate mother or an aunt" (p. 179). And finally, the 'daughter complex', which takes the form of the young woman's longing for a father figure. Gu draws on examples from Chinese literature and stories that indicate the existence of these individual complexes, where Oedipal feelings are displaced onto similar or disguised objects. Gu argues that in Chinese culture, the Oedipus complex is fragmented, describing it as a "*muted complex*" (p. 189; italics in original) or a "filial piety complex" (p. 163).

These are only a small number of explorations of other cultural myths, but they suggest how the themes of incestuous desire, jealousy and rivalry, and triangular parent–child dynamics are a repeated theme.

Oedipal Dynamics in Families Across Culture

A third method for exploring the universality of the Oedipal complex might be to study how Oedipal dynamics may occur in families across cultural contexts. However, such research is made complicated in that it requires an operational definition of the Oedipus complex, and as we have seen in previous chapters, there are many differing interpretations. Thus, cross-cultural research on the Oedipus complex is methodologically and conceptually problematic.

Barnaby Barratt (2019) suggests that in approaching the consideration of the Oedipus complex as universal, there has been a tendency to focus on the content of the individual's Oedipal story, the arrangements of the family, the parents and the practices of caretaking of a child, which have been found to vary cross-culturally. Instead, he suggests a need to focus on the "*processes* and *structures* of oedipality", which he argues to be "indisputably universal" (p. 8). He distinguishes between Oedipal *complexes*, which vary across individuals, and '*Oedipality*', which is a metapsychological construct that involves the child's necessary encounter with, and negotiation of, the incest taboo. For example, a focus is often on the content of the role of 'mother' and 'father' in the Oedipus complexes, rather than the processes of the 'maternal function' and 'paternal function', which Barratt highlights are processes that could be performed by a man or a woman. Barratt describes the sensuous, erotic bond between the child and caregiver, within which, over time, the child must come to discover and accept that some aspects of this bond involve forbidden erotic desires which the child cannot have indulged; a taboo which is delivered by the paternal function (regardless of the gender of the person performing this role). As he describes: "Children have an intense and ubiquitously erotic bond with their early caretakers, but later 'discover' that certain sorts of erotic activities are profoundly forbidden in relation to the very individuals with whom they are most attached" (2019, p. 14).

Barratt argues that Oedipal complexes arise out of Oedipality, which is universal. Oedipality is negotiated in various ways and is experienced as varying complexes, involving sexuality, relationships, and limitations.

We should also consider the cultural variations with regards notions of the self and experience of the self and relationships. Often this is discussed with reference to differences between what have been termed 'collectivist' versus 'individualist' cultures (Hofstede, 1984). In individualist cultures, such as in North America and many societies of Europe, the emphasis is on the self as an independent individual, whereas in collectivist cultures, such as many societies in Asia and Africa, the self cannot be considered as independent from the family or community. In collectivist cultures the self is more aligned with a sense of 'we-ness', a familial self, whereas in individualist cultures, the self is more aligned with a sense of 'I-ness', an individualised self (Roland, 1984). Hofstede's conceptualisation of individualist versus collectivist dimensions of culture has been critiqued for equating whole nations with culture and ignoring the multiculturalism within nations and societies (e.g. McSweeney, 2002), and indeed, families. In contemporary society, these dimensions are more blurred. Yet, these differences can still be observed and are reflected in some of the cross-cultural studies of Oedipal myths discussed above, such as those described by Gu (2006).

The notion of a familial self is reflected in Kenichiro Okano's (2018) description of a typical Japanese family situation and his consideration of the relevance of this for the Oedipus complex. In collectivist cultures, there is typically an expectation of loyalty and deference towards authority and the group. Okano describes Japanese fathers as more involved in the world of work, less possessive of their wives, with young children typically kept close to their parents sleeping in the same room. He suggests that while fathers are disciplinary, they are not seemingly threatened by the child's close attachment to the mother, thus do not present as a castrating figure. However, fathers tend to be under the fear of castration in the workplace where submission to authority is often expected. Okana suggests that the scrutinising, castrating authority is not so much the father, but rather the *collective*; Japanese society. He points out how a self-effacing attitude and a degree of shame is valued and promoted in Japanese culture, whereas majority cultures in Europe and North America tend to devalue such qualities, encouraging instead the demonstration of *individual* strength and capability. In Japanese culture, power, as represented by the phallus, is something to be concealed, rather than acquired and made visible. This in turn prevents envy in others. The Japanese cultural taboos around intrusion and exposure manifest in behaviours of non-expression or secretiveness, and passivity, such as not looking or staring at someone. The uncovering of perceived weakness or flaws in others is taboo. He concludes that the Oedipal taboo in Japan is not so much hostility towards the father, who is perceived as a rival, but rather "the taboo is to challenge the hidden or unwritten rules that govern society" (Okano, 2018, p. 1360).

In terms of a nuclear family, we might say that there is typically a basic triadic structure of child, primary caregiver, usually the mother, and another caregiver, usually the child's father or primary caregiver's partner. There are other adults and children often involved, of course. Across cultures we may have this basic triadic structure, with the inevitable psychological conflicts involving feelings of love and jealousy, and experiences of inclusion or exclusion. However, the particular emotional dynamics of the relationships between these three figures may be influenced by the cultural context.

Chapter 9

Oedipus Now

What is the Oedipus complex, and is it still relevant? This is a question that is asked repeatedly. Many will say it is indeed still of significance. Many others will say it is a myth and fantasy that has no place in understanding human psychology and sexuality. As Freud astutely observed, it is a theory that divides opinion. In this final chapter, I offer some thoughts in an attempt to bring together some of the different perspectives covered in previous chapters and also consider some more recent contributions coming from neuroscience.

As we have seen through the various theories and perspectives offered, what has been referred to as 'the Oedipus complex' is many things. It is a model for how the incest taboo is established, and consequently morality, ethics, and law, in the mind of the child. It is a model for understanding the unbridled expressions of the child's instincts, and how these become tamed over the course of his or her psychic development. It is a model for understanding the formation and development of gender and sexual identity. It is a model for how the child must separate developmentally from their parents and establish an independent life of their own, with all the intense feelings that this evokes. It is a model of triangulated relationships which the child must navigate through with regards their sense of themselves in relation to their parents. The Oedipus complex is primarily about the father and his authority. It is primarily about the mother and her mothering. It is about the primal scene and the parental couple. The Oedipus complex is phylogenetically inherited. It is repressed in the unconscious mind

DOI: 10.4324/9781003394471-9

of the individual. It is an Oedipus 'situation' that exists as a structure into which the child is born. It is a social and cultural narrative and structure for the ordering of society and the establishment of authority. It can seem to be all these things, and more.

Christopher Bollas (1996) makes the interesting suggestion that the psychoanalytic profession is engaged in theoretical debates that 'break' the Oedipal triangle, by attempting to either "kick out the mother", with an emphasis on the father and the phallus, or "kick out the father", with an emphasis on the mother and the maternal breasts (p. 6). He suggests that the psychoanalytic profession itself has an Oedipus complex that it struggles to resolve, constantly marginalising or killing off a parent in favour of another.

Part of the difficulty is that there are certain theoretical tensions that are consistently grappled with. One major tension exists between the demarcation of what is biological, what is social, and what is cultural. Is sexuality determined by biological sex, or is it social and cultural, or both? Is sexuality about function and procreation, or is it about desire and pleasure? Is sexuality orientated to an object or is it disorientated? Is it more about 'nature' or is it more about 'nurture'? These are realms of influence that psychoanalysis (and not only psychoanalysis) has struggled to demarcate. Freud himself grappled with some of these tensions, on the one hand understanding sexuality to be disorientated, and driven by pleasure, and on the other hand providing an account of sexuality that was more organised and leaned on Darwinian ideas of procreation (Van Haute & Westerink, 2020).

As a neurologist, and keen to establish his new psychoanalytic theory as a science, Freud grounded his theories of sexuality, and the Oedipus complex, in biology. Yet, he also acknowledged the social and cultural dimensions of sexuality. Since Freud, psychoanalytic theory has shifted from a more biological and intrapsychic understanding of human development and the human mind to a more relational, developmental focus. However, we are biological creatures. Freud did not have the scientific tools of investigation that we have today to support some of his claims, so he recognised that at times he could only make hypotheses. Mark Solms (mentioned in Chapter 8) has brought some neuroscientific evidence to correct some of Freud's theories, but not dismiss them. He provides an interesting, and I think very helpful, contemporary biological formulation of the Oedipus complex.

Solms (2018) suggests that what Freud referred to as the drives of the id (sexuality and aggressive drives) are expressed as innate biological needs that are felt as emotional and bodily affects. He refers to the taxonomy of basic emotional drives identified by the neuroscientist, Jaak Panksepp, suggesting that rather than only two biological needs, we are born with seven innate biological emotional drives, which are: the need to engage with the world (expressed as the drive of SEEKING); the need to escape danger (felt as FEAR); the need for attachment (the absence of which is felt as PANIC-GRIEF); the need to attack against frustration (felt as RAGE); the need to find sexual partners (felt as LUST); the need to nurture others (the CARE drive); and, finally, the need to PLAY.

As discussed in Chapter 8, Freud (1913) understood the male child's sexual attraction to his mother as conflicting with two innate, evolutionary-biological dispositions – castration anxiety and the taboo of incest – which exist as inherited 'primal phantasies' in the unconscious. Solms (2021) argues that the Oedipus complex, as Freud understood it, cannot be an inherited innate biological disposition, given what we know from neuroscience about memory and the brain. However, he offers a revision of the biological origins and basis of the Oedipus complex, which he formulates as involving a constellation of innate biological needs and emotional responses. He states:

> Not only must the child reconcile its LUST with its attachment bonds; it must do so in the context of the RAGE aroused by the frustration of these needs, as well as the PANIC that this in turn gives rise to in relation to the caregiver (and hence to guilt), but also the FEAR that is aroused by the RAGE that is felt toward the frustrating parent standing between the child and the object of its LUST, and so on. All of these competing, heartfelt emotions – which are inevitably felt toward the child's primary objects – must somehow be reconciled with each other. This is the Oedipus complex.
>
> (Solms, 2021, pp. 570–571)

The child must find ways of meeting this set of biological needs, made difficult in that they are in conflict with one another, and, importantly, in conflict with the need demands of the parents, and other individuals (e.g. siblings). They can only be mastered through relational experience. Solms states that an important element here, for children learning to manage these demands, is the biological emotional need of PLAY. It is through the 'as-if' nature of play that children learn socially accepted behaviours and limits, and the interpersonal qualities of mutuality and respect for the needs of others. He suggests that it is PLAY that "underscores the incest taboo" (2021, p. 575). A parent may thus allow the child to PLAY at being 'mommy's little man' but sets a limit on *actually* being her partner.

This provides a compelling biological model of the Oedipus complex, grounded in contemporary neuroscientific evidence, describing the intense biological needs and feelings that the child must navigate, manage, and tame, in relation to his or her parents (regardless of their gender). These are the emotional conflicts and dynamics described in different ways across all the various formulations discussed in this book – the intense feelings of love, envy, and rivalry felt towards the parents. Solms presents us with a biological basis for the Oedipus complex, upon which, we might say, is layered a familial, social and cultural Oedipal narrative or structure, that shapes the child's developing sexuality. That is, narratives consciously and unconsciously communicated that the child receives as messages about who he or she is, their relationship to his or her parents, their place in the world when a child and when an adult, what it means to be a man and a woman, what are deemed sexually appropriate behaviours, and who they should preferably be sexually intimate with. Such messages are internalised to form part of the mind and personality and shape the emerging sexuality of the child. In the mix too, are the unconscious and conscious fantasies that the naive child forms to help them attempt to make sense of the confusing adult world, and adult relationships, and their place in it.

In a similar way to how Freud has repeatedly been declared 'dead' and yet is still found to be of interest, relevance, and importance, so too the Oedipus complex. A dogmatic adherence to an Oedipus 'simplex' model that only casts females as 'lacking' a phallus, and that tends to moralise sexuality and gender that does not adhere to a heterosexual norm, has been problematic in the past. Many find it easy to accuse Freud for past problematic applications of the Oedipus complex and understanding of sexuality and gender. However, as we saw in Chapter 2, he was at times much more open to variability and possibilities, and his ideas on innate bisexuality and the 'complete' Oedipus complex are influential in contemporary psychoanalytic approaches. Solms' model, I think, complements this. Contemporary psychoanalysis pays more attention to the varying same-sex and cross-sex desires, and the conflicting wishes, fantasies, jealousies, and hostilities roused by the triangular relationship that a child finds themselves in, and has to navigate their way through, so as to find their place within family, adult relationships, and society, balancing their emotional needs as well as the emotional needs of others. These echo the conflicts and dynamics of a sexual and relational nature experienced in adulthood that we see in our consulting rooms again and again. The Oedipus complex continues to provide us with a helpful framework for understanding these.

References

The abbreviation SE refers in this book to *The Standard Edition of the Complete Psychological Works of Sigmund Freud*, J. Strachey, Trans. and General Ed. London: Hogarth Press.

Aron, L. (1995). The internalized primal scene. *Psychoanalytic Dialogues*, 5(2), 195–237.

Bailly, L. (2009). *Lacan*. Oxford: Oneworld Publications.

Balsam, R. H. (2015). Oedipus Rex: Where are we going, especially with females? *The Psychoanalytic Quarterly*, 84(3), 555–588.

Barratt, B. B. (2019). Oedipality and oedipal complexes reconsidered: On the incest taboo as key to the universality of the human condition. *The International Journal of Psychoanalysis*, 100(1), 7–31.

Benjamin, J. (1988). *The bonds of love: Psychoanalysis, feminism and the problem of domination*. New York: Pantheon Books.

Benjamin, J. (1998). *Shadow of the other: Intersubjectivity and gender in psychoanalysis*. Abingdon: Routledge.

Bion, W. (1959). Attacks on linking. *International Journal of Psychoanalysis*, 40, 308–315.

Bollas, C. (1996). Figures and their functions: On the Oedipal structure of a psychoanalysis. *The Psychoanalytic Quarterly*, 65(1), 1–20.

Britton, R. (1989). The missing link: Parental sexuality in the Oedipus complex. In J. Steiner (Ed.), *The Oedipus complex today: Clinical implications* (pp. 83–101). London: Karnac Books.

Britton, R. (1992). The Oedipus situation and the depressive position. In R. Anderson (Ed.), *Clinical lectures on Klein and Bion* (pp. 34–45). Hove: Routledge.

Butler, J. (1990). *Gender trouble*. New York: Routledge.

Chasseguet-Smirgel, J. (1976). Freud and female sexuality: The considera-tion of some blind spots in the exploration of the "Dark Continent". *The International Journal of Psychoanalysis*, 57(3), 275–286.

Chasseguet-Smirgel, J. (1988). From the archaic matrix of the Oedipus complex to the fully developed Oedipus complex: Theoretical perspec-tive in relation to clinical experience and technique. *The Psychoanalytic Quarterly*, 57(4), 505–527.

Chasseguet-Smirgel, J. (1989). *Sexuality and mind: The role of the father and the mother in the psyche*. London: Karnac Books.

Chodorow, N. J. (1978). *The reproduction of mothering: Psychoanalysis and the sociology of gender*. Los Angeles: University of California Press.

Chodorow, N. J. (1992). Heterosexuality as a compromise formation: Reflections on the psychoanalytic theory of sexual development. *Psychoanalysis and Contemporary Thought*, 15(3), 267–304.

Chodorow, N. J. (2012). *Individualizing gender and sexuality: Theory and practice*. New York: Routledge.

Corbett, K. (1993). The mystery of homosexuality. *Psychoanalytic Psychology*, 10(3), 345–357.

Corbett, K. (2001). Nontraditional family romance. *The Psychoanalytic Quarterly*, 70(3), 599–624.

Corbett, K. (2008). Gender now. *Psychoanalytic Dialogues*, 18(6), 838–856.

Davies, J. M. (2003). Falling in love with love: Oedipal and postoedipal manifestations of idealization, mourning, and erotic masochism. *Psy-choanalytic Dialogues*, 13(1), 1–27.

Davies, J. M. (2015). From Oedipus complex to Oedipal complexity: Reconfiguring (pardon the expression) the negative Oedipus complex and the disowned erotics of disowned sexualities. *Psychoanalytic Dialogues*, 25 (3), 265–283.

Dimen, M. (1999). Between *lust* and libido: Sex, psychoanalysis, and the moment before. *Psychoanalytic Dialogues*, 9(4), 415–440.

Eitan-Persico, Y. (2024). *Oedipal experiences in same-sex families*. Abingdon: Routledge.

Elise, D. (1997). Primary femininity, bisexuality, and the female ego ideal: A re-examination of female developmental theory. *The Psychoanalytic Quarterly*, 66(3), 489–517.

Elise, D. (1998). The absence of the paternal penis. *Journal of the American Psychoanalytic Association*, 46(2), 413–442.

Elise, D. (2000). Woman and desire: Why women may not want to want. *Studies in Gender and Sexuality*, 1(2), 125–145.

Elise, D. (2002). The primary maternal Oedipal situation and female homoerotic desire. *Psychoanalytic Inquiry*, 22(2), 209–228.

Fast, I. (1978). Developments in gender identity: The original matrix. *International Review of Psychoanalysis*, 5, 265–273.

Fast, I. (1979). Developments in gender identity: Gender differentiation in girls. *The International Journal of Psychoanalysis*, 60, 443–453.

Fast, I. (1990). Aspects of early gender development: Toward a reformulation. *Psychoanalytic Psychology*, 7(Suppl.), 105–117.

Freud, S. (1905). Three essays on the theory of sexuality. *SE*, VII.

Freud, S. (1909). Analysis of a phobia in a five-year-old boy. *SE*, X.

Freud, S. (1910). Leonardo da Vinci and a memory of his childhood. *SE*, XI.

Freud, S. (1913). Totem and taboo. *SE*, XIII.

Freud, S. (1918). From the history of an infantile neurosis. *SE*, XVII.

Freud, S. (1920). The psychogenesis of a case of female homosexuality. *SE*, XVIII.

Freud, S. (1923). The ego and the id. *SE*, XIX.

Freud, S. (1924). The dissolution of the Oedipus complex. *SE*, XIX.

Freud, S. (1925). Some psychical consequences of the anatomical distinction between the sexes. *SE*, XIX.

Freud, S. (1926). The question of lay analysis. *SE*, XX.

Freud, S. (1931). Female sexuality. *SE*, XXI.

Gabbard, G. O. & Gabbard, K. (1999). *Psychiatry and the cinema* (2nd ed.). Washington, DC: American Psychiatric Press.

Giffney, N. & Watson, E. (Eds.) (2017). *Clinical encounters in sexuality: Psychoanalytic practice and queer theory*. New York: Punctum Books.

Goldsmith, S. J. (1995). Oedipus or Orestes? Aspects of gender identity development in homosexual men. *Psychoanalytic Inquiry*, 15(1), 112–124.

Goldsmith, S. J. (2001). Oedipus or Orestes? Homosexual men, their mothers, and other women revisited. *Journal of the American Psychoanalytic Association*, 49(4), 1269–1287.

Green, A. (1995). Has sexuality anything to do with psychoanalysis? *International Journal of Psychoanalysis*, 76, 871–884.

Green, A. (2004). Thirdness and psychoanalytic concepts. *The Psychoanalytic Quarterly*, 73(1), 99–135.

Gu, M. D. (2006). The filial piety complex: Variations on the Oedipus theme in Chinese literature and culture. *The Psychoanalytic Quarterly*, 75(1), 163–195.

Hägglund, T. B. & Hägglund, V. (1981). The boy who killed his father and wed his mother: The Oedipus theme in Finnish folklore. *International Review of Psychoanalysis*, 8(1), 53–62.

Harris, A. (2009). *Gender as soft assembly*. New York: Routledge.

Hartke, R. (2016). The Oedipus complex: A confrontation at the central cross-roads of psychoanalysis. *The International Journal of Psychoanalysis*, 97(3), 893–913.

Heenen-Wolff, S. (2011). Infantile bisexuality and the 'complete Oedipal complex': Freudian views on heterosexuality and homosexuality. *The International Journal of Psychoanalysis*, 92(5), 1209–1220.

Hertzmann, L. & Newbigin, J. (2023). *Psychoanalysis and homosexuality: A contemporary introduction*. Abingdon: Routledge.

Hofstede, G. (1984). *Culture's consequences: International differences in work-related values*. Newbury Park: Sage Publications.

Horney, K. (1924). On the genesis of the castration complex in women. *The International Journal of Psychoanalysis*, 5, 50–65.

Horney, K. (1926). The flight from womanhood: The masculinity complex in women as viewed by men and by women. *The International Journal of Psychoanalysis*, 7, 324–339.

Horney, K. (1932). The dread of woman. *The International Journal of Psychoanalysis*, 13, 348–360.

Horney, K. (1933). The denial of the vagina. *The International Journal of Psychoanalysis*, 14, 57–70.

Isay, R. A. (1986). The development of sexual identity in homosexual men. *The Psychoanalytic Study of the Child*, 41(1), 467–489.

Isay, R. A. (1987). Fathers and their homosexually inclined sons in childhood. *The Psychoanalytic Study of the Child*, 42(1), 275–294.

Josephs, L. (2011). The primal scene in cross-species and cross-cultural perspectives. *The International Journal of Psychoanalysis*, 92(5), 1263–1287.

Kakar, S. (1989). The maternal-feminine in Indian psychoanalysis. *International Review of Psychoanalysis*, 16(3), 355–362.

Klein, M. (1928). Early stages of the Oedipus conflict. *The International Journal of Psychoanalysis*, 9, 167–180.

Klein, M. (1930). The importance of symbol formation in the development of the ego. In *The Writings of Melanie Klein, Vol. 1* (pp. 219–232). London: Hogarth Press.

Klein, M. (1932). *The Psychoanalysis of children*. London: Hogarth Press.

Klein, M. (1935). A contribution to the psychogenesis of manic-depressive states. *International Journal of Psychoanalysis*, 16, 145–174.

Klein, M. (1945). The Oedipus complex in the light of early anxieties. *The International Journal of Psychoanalysis*, 26, 11–33.

Klein, M. (1946). Notes on some schizoid mechanisms. *International Journal of Psychoanalysis*, 27, 99–110.

Klein, M. (1959). Our adult world and its roots in infancy. *Human Relations*, 12(4), 291–303.

Kulish, N. & Holtzman, D. (2008). *A story of her own: The female Oedipus complex reexamined and renamed*. Maryland: Jason Aronson.

Lacan, J. (2001). *Ecrits: A selection*. Abingdon: Routledge.

Laplanche, J. (1976). *Life and death in psychoanalysis*. Baltimore: John Hopkins University Press.

Laplanche, J. (2011). *Freud and the sexual*. New York: International Psychoanalytic Books.

Lemma, A. (2017). *The digital age on the couch: Psychoanalytic practice and new media*. London: Routledge.

Lévi-Strauss, C. (1969). *The elementary structures of kinship* (Revised edition; translated from the French). Boston: Beacon Press.

Lewes, K. (1988). *The psychoanalytic theory of male homosexuality*. New York: New American Library.

Lewes, K. (1998). A special Oedipal mechanism in the development of male homosexuality. *Psychoanalytic Psychology*, 15(3), 341–359.

Lingiardi, V. & Carone, N. (2019). Challenging Oedipus in changing families: Gender identifications and access to origins in same-sex parent families created through third-party reproduction. *The International Journal of Psychoanalysis*, 100(2), 229–246.

Loewald, H. W. (1979). The waning of the Oedipus complex. *Journal of the American Psychoanalytic Association*, 27(4), 751–775.

Loewald, H. W. (1985). Oedipus complex and development of self. *The Psychoanalytic Quarterly*, 54(3), 435–443.

Luepnitz, D. A. (2019). Oedipus simplex: The British blind spot. *Couple and Family Psychoanalysis*, 9(2), ix–xii.

Luepnitz, D. A. (2021). A return to Freud's 'complete Oedipus complex': Reclaiming the negative. *American Imago*, 78(4), 619–630.

Malinowski, B. (1927/2001). *Sex and repression in savage society*. London: Routledge.

Masson, J. M. (Ed.) (1985). *The complete letters of Sigmund Freud to Wilhelm Fliess, 1887–1904*. Cambridge: The Belknap Press of Harvard University Press.

Mayer, E. L. (1985). 'Everybody must be just like me': Observations on female castration anxiety. *The International Journal of Psychoanalysis*, 66, 331–347.

McDougall, J. (1995). *The many faces of eros: A psychoanalytic exploration of human sexuality*. London: Free Association Books.

McSweeney, B. (2002). Hofstede's model of national cultural differences and their consequences: A triumph of faith-a failure of analysis. *Human Relations*, 55(1), 89–118.

Mitchell, J. (1974). *Feminism and psychoanalysis*. London: Allen Lane.

Money-Kyrle, R. (1971). The aim of psychoanalysis. *The International Journal of Psychoanalysis*, 52(1), 103–106.

Nathans, S. (2021). Oedipus for everyone: Revitalizing the model for LGBTQ couples and single parent families. *Psychoanalytic Dialogues*, 31(3), 312–328.

O'Connor, F. (1933/2005). *My Oedipus complex and other stories*. London: Penguin.

O'Connor, N. & Ryan, J. (1993). *Wild desires and mistaken identities. Lesbianism and psychoanalysis*. London: Karnac Books.

Ogden, T. H. (1989). *The primitive edge of experience*. New Jersey: Jason Aronson.

Okano, K. (2018). Passivity, non-expression and the Oedipus in Japan. *The International Journal of Psychoanalysis*, 99(6), 1353–1365.

Perelberg, R. J. (2015). *Murdered father, dead father: Revisiting the Oedipus complex*. Abingdon: Routledge.

Perelberg, R. J. (2018). Introduction: A psychoanalytic understanding of psychic bisexuality. In R. J. Perelberg (Ed.), *Psychic bisexuality: A British-French dialogue* (pp. 1–57). Abingdon: Routledge.

Rohleder, P. (2020). Homophobia, heteronormativity and shame. In L. Hertzmann & J. Newbigin (Eds.), *Sexuality and gender now: Looking beyond heteronormativity* (pp. 40–56). Abingdon: Routledge.

Rohleder, P. (2025). Homophobia, heteronormativity and melancholia: A psychoanalytic essay on the film All of Us Strangers. *International Journal of Psychoanalysis*. doi:10.1080/00207578.2024.2402901.

Roland, A. (1984). Psychoanalysis in civilizational perspective: The self in India, Japan, and America. *Psychoanalytic Review*, 71(4), 569–590.

Rusbridger, R. (2004). Elements of the Oedipus complex: A Kleinian account. *The International Journal of Psychoanalysis*, 85(3), 731–748.

Scarfone, D. (2013). A brief introduction to the work of Jean Laplanche. *The International Journal of Psychoanalysis*, 94(3), 545–566.

Schafer, R. (2002). On male nonnormative sexuality and perversion in psychoanalytic discourse. *Annual of Psychoanalysis*, 30, 23–35.

Solms, M. (2018). The neurobiological underpinnings of psychoanalytic theory and therapy. *Frontiers in Behavioral Neuroscience*, 12, article 294.

Solms, M. (2021). A revision of Freud's theory of the biological origin of the Oedipus complex. *The Psychoanalytic Quarterly*, 90(4), 555–581.

Spiro, M. (1982/2010). *Oedipus in the Trobriands*. New Brunswick: Transaction Publishers.

Stein, R. (1990). A new look at the theory of Melanie Klein. *The International Journal of Psychoanalysis*, 71, 499–511.

Stein, R. (1998a). The enigmatic dimension of sexual experience: The "otherness" of sexuality and primal seduction. *The Psychoanalytic Quarterly*, 67(4), 594–625.

Stein, R. (1998b). The poignant, the excessive and the enigmatic in sexuality. *The International Journal of Psychoanalysis*, 79(2), 253–268.

Steiner, J. (1985). Turning a blind eye: The cover up for Oedipus. *International Review of Psychoanalysis*, 12(2), 161–172.

Steiner, J. (1990). The retreat from truth to omnipotence in Sophocles' Oedipus at Colonus. *International Review of Psychoanalysis*, 17(2), 227–237.

Steiner, J. (1996). Revenge and resentment in the 'Oedipus situation'. *International Journal of Psychoanalysis*, 77(3), 433–443.

Steiner, J. (1999). The struggle for dominance in the Oedipus situation. *Canadian Journal of Psychoanalysis*, 7(2), 161–177.

Steiner, J. (2018). The trauma and disillusionment of Oedipus. *The International Journal of Psychoanalysis*, 99(3), 555–568.

Stoller, R. J. (1968). *Sex and gender: The development of masculinity and femininity.* London: Karnac.

Tang, N. M. & Smith, B. L. (1996). The eternal triangle across cultures: Oedipus, Hsueh, and Ganesa. *The Psychoanalytic Study of the Child*, 51(1), 562–579.

Van Haute, P. & Westerink, H. (2020). *Reading Freud's three essays on the theory of sexuality: From pleasure to the object.* Abingdon: Routledge.

Winnicott, D. W. (1953). Transitional objects and transitional phenomena – A study of the first not-me possession. *International Journal of Psychoanalysis*, 34, 89–97.

Winnicott, D. W. (1965). *The maturational processes and the facilitating environment.* London: Hogarth Press.

Winnicott, D. W. (1967). Mirror-role of mother and family in child development. In P. Lomas (Ed.), *The predicament of the family: A psycho-analytic symposium* (pp. 26–33). London: Hogarth Press.

Winnicott, D. W. (1969). The use of an object. *International Journal of Psychoanalysis*, 50, 711–716.

Yadlin-Gadot, S. & Hadar, U. (2023). *Lacanian psychoanalysis: A contemporary introduction.* Abingdon: Routledge.

Zepf, S. & Seel, D. (2016). Penis envy and the female Oedipus complex: A plea to reawaken an ineffectual debate. *The Psychoanalytic Review*, 103(3), 397–421.

Zepf, S., Ullrich, B. & Seel, D. (2016). Oedipus and the Oedipus complex: A revision. *The International Journal of Psychoanalysis*, 97(3), 685–707.

Index

Adult-infans relationship
   (Laplanche) 59–61
Aron, Lewis 32–33, 77, 87, 99

Barratt, Barnaby 110–111
Benjamin, Jessica 34, 43, 66,
   71–77, 87
Bion, Wilfred 29
Bisexual matrix 42, 95
Britton, Ronald 28–32, 57
Butler, Judith 77, 87

Castrated mother/woman 12, 14,
   36, 38, 89
Castration anxiety 5, 8–14, 18–19,
   34–41, 43, 70, 80, 101, 107, 108,
   115
Chasseguet-Smirgel, Janine 18, 23,
   38, 51, 69, 80
Chodorow, Nancy 34, 46, 66–71,
   75
Combined parent figure (Klein)
   20, 24–27, 28, 32–33, 82
Complete Oedipus complex 4, 7,
   16–18, 41, 62, 89, 94–97, 117
Corbett, Ken 87, 88, 99
Cross-cultural Oedipal myths
   107–110

Davies, Jody Messler 77, 83–84,
   97–99

Depressive position 20–24, 26–27,
   28–32, 79
Drives16, 23, 57, 72, 115; sexual
   drive 57–62

Elise, Dianne 39, 43, 44, 50, 95–96
Enigmatic sexuality 19, 40, 57–63, 81

Family romance 99–100, 119
Fast, Irene 41–43, 76, 95
Freud, Sigmund 1–6, 7–19, 21, 24,
   27, 30, 34, 35, 37, 38, 40–43, 45,
   51, 54, 59–63, 65, 68, 71, 73, 75,
   78, 80, 81, 86, 87–90, 94, 97, 98,
   99, 101–103, 104–108, 113, 114,
   115, 117
Fundamental anthropological
   situation (Laplanche) 59, 61–62

Gender differentiation 41–43, 76
Gender identity 39, 61, 63, 87, 89,
   96, 113
Green, André 56–57, 65, 81

Heenen-Wolff, Susann 18, 96
Holtzman, Deanna 43, 45–47, 50
Homosexuality 5, 10, 12–13,
   15–16, 33, 37, 64, 86, 87,
   88–92, 95, 96, 97, 100; homoerotic desire 84–85, 88, 90,
   95, 96, 98–99, 119; same-sex

desire 4, 5, 27, 63, 86–88, 94–99, 117
Horney, Karen 21, 35–38, 39, 40, 41, 50, 63, 69, 80

Incest taboo 2, 3, 5, 8, 9, 11, 14, 41, 56, 62, 83, 101–108, 110, 113, 115, 116
Infantile sexuality 7–9, 58–62, 78, 97
Instincts 7–9, 13, 2, 22, 24, 27, 37, 57–60, 62, 71, 102, 113
Internalised parental couple 28–29, 32, 84
Intersubjectivity 32, 68, 72–77
Isay, Richard 88, 90–92, 94, 96, 98

Klein, Melanie 4, 20–33, 36, 53, 63, 65, 69, 77, 79, 82
Kulish, Nancy 43, 45–47, 50

Lacan, Jaques 4, 51–57
Laplanche, Jean 4, 19, 40, 51, 57–63, 81, 96
Lewes, Kenneth 12, 88–90, 94
Little Hans (case study) 12, 38, 42
Loewald, Hans 77–79, 83, 84
Luepnitz, Deborah 18, 94, 96, 97

McDougall, Joyce 51, 63–64
Malinowksi, Bronislaw 101, 103–106
Maternal Oedipus situation 44
Mayer, Elizabeth 39
Mitchell, Juliet 40, 54
Monosexuality 63–64

Oedipal complexity 83–84, 87
Oedipal situation 5, 20–21, 28–31, 44, 47, 57, 69
Oedipality 110–111
Ogden, Thomas 77, 79–82

Paranoid schizoid position 22–24, 25, 28, 30, 31, 32, 80
Parricide 78–79, 83, 108–109
Part-object 22, 26

Paternal function 56, 57, 110
Paternal Oedipus situation 44
Patriarchy 40, 104
Penis envy 14, 18–19, 34–38, 39, 40–41, 42, 63, 75–76
Perelberg, Rosine 51, 56, 57, 102
Persephone complex 43, 45–47
Phallic stage 8, 10, 14, 21, 37, 63, 89
Phallus 13, 40, 54–56, 68, 78, 89, 112, 114, 117; phallus as signifier of loss 54–55
Plicate Oedipus complex 89–90
Polymorphously perverse sexuality 7, 9, 24, 97
Pre-Oedipal period 37, 54, 65, 68–70, 80, 82, 89
Primal horde 9, 54, 101–102
Primal scene 13, 21, 24, 30, 32–33, 82–83, 99, 104–105, 113
Primary femininity 16, 39, 40, 95–96
Primary Oedipal configurations 98–99
Psychic bisexuality/innate bisexuality 4, 5, 7, 13, 15, 16–18, 41, 44, 63, 86, 89, 94–98, 117
Psychosexual stages 7–10, 59, 73

Queer theory 86–88

Repudiation of femininity 15, 75

Same-sex families 99–100
Secondary Oedipal configurations 98–99
Solms, Mark 6, 57, 107, 114–117
Spiro, Melford 101, 105–107
Stein, Ruth 27–28, 61, 63
Steiner, John 28, 29–31

Transitional Oedipal relationship (Ogden) 79–83
Triangular space 29, 30, 32, 82
Trobriand Islanders 103–106

Winnicott, Donald 52, 67, 74, 79, 80

For Product Safety Concerns and Information please contact our EU
representative GPSR@taylorandfrancis.com
Taylor & Francis Verlag GmbH, Kaufingerstraße 24, 80331 München, Germany

www.ingramcontent.com/pod-product-compliance
Lightning Source LLC
Chambersburg PA
CBHW070348270326
41926CB00017B/4039